Unveiling Jesus: 144 Days of Revelation

144 Reflections on Jesus' Identity and Mission

(with topical and Scripture index)

By W. Bascom Moore

© 2025 Spiritbuilding Publishers.

All rights reserved. No part of this book may be reproduced in any form without the written permission of the publisher.

Published by
Spiritbuilding Publishers
9700 Ferry Road, Waynesville, OH 45068

Unveiling Jesus: *144 Days of Revelation*
  144 Reflections on Jesus' Identity and Mission

by W. Bascom Moore

ISBN: 9781955285858

Table of Contents

Acknowledgments 1
Introduction 2
The Devotionals Begin 6
Addendum 218
Index of Verses 220
Outline of Topics 227
Index of Topics 228

Acknowledgments

I have endeavored to limit my observations to what is found in the scriptures. Since the inspired writers were guided by the Holy Spirit, I defer to His authority as I am able. If you sense that one of my points is not supported by the text, within context, then it is fair to call it into question.

> "Everyone who goes on ahead and does not abide in the teaching of Christ, does not have God. Whoever abides in the teaching has both the Father and the Son." *2 John 1:9*

My most foundational acknowledgment is God. That follows since the purpose of this book is to amplify the voice of the Holy Spirit on key topics about the person of Jesus Christ.

Special thanks are due to my wife and chief editor, Lynne Moore. Roger Clevenger helped brainstorm with me on these subjects. Those who directed me to some of the passages include Dennis Faulkner, Bob Koors, Greg Tidwell, and David Moore. I am so grateful for R.M., who has acted as my foil in challenging my understanding of the scriptures; he has motivated me in moving to a much deeper understanding of God's word than I would have without him.

Introduction

Veils

There are so many veils hiding Jesus from our hearts and minds. I intend that this book aid in removing such veils from our senses. This process consists of removing obstacles which prevent a relationship with Jesus or hinder the growth of our current relationship. To set your expectations, here are three types of veils which these devotionals can address:

- Veils of Prejudice: prejudging Jesus based on hearsay anecdotes that we've never bothered to scrutinize
- Veils of Ignorance: being neither opposed to Jesus nor promoting Him, but lacking motivation to approach Jesus by reason of our ignorance about his kingship and his church
- Veils of Complacency: These are very difficult to lift, requiring one to be reborn—opening our eyes to see Jesus as if for the very first time
- Veil of Your Journey: Your own experiences will color your own ability to understand the message of Jesus

By reducing the number of veils, we will discover the very aweinspiring Jesus, one to be feared, revered, and loved.

Methodology

Each devotional was sought out to highlight the nature of Jesus's person and the nature of his work. His person encompasses his deity and kingship. His work centers on the cross: his death, resurrection, and the purchase of his church. Devotional passages are catalogued in eight themes, accessed via a detailed topical index at the end.

Themes

Each devotional presents passages focusing our attention on one or more of these eight aspects of Jesus's person and work.
1. Jesus's Divinity
2. Purpose of the Cross
3. Cross Plan
4. Predictions of His Death, Burial, and Resurrection

5. Premeditated Crucifixion
6. Essential Cross
7. New Covenant
8. Kingdom of Heaven

In most cases, I avoid extensive commentary. I point out a couple of highlights from the above list of subjects upon which the passage sheds light. Each passage says much more than I point out. The reader is left to notice these on his own and meditate on what else the Holy Spirit has to say. My goal is to draw his attention to the passage, pique her interest, challenge his thinking. But those who are seeking verses and devotionals on these themes can utilize the topical index at the end.

Origins of the Book

I had been talking with my cousin R.M. He is in a religious group which denies many elements of Christianity. The eight selected points are a response to all that I have learned in my many discussions with R.M. spanning over fourteen years. Here is a list of corresponding counterpoints gleaned from the teachings of R.M. and his religion:

1. Jesus was not divine, nor did he create the world.
2. The Cross was not God's purpose.
3. The Cross was merely a backup plan after God's" "Plan A" failed to materialize.
4. Predictions of the cross are merely predictions of the backup plan, "Plan "B".
5. The Cross was essentially an afterthought, rather than premeditated by God.
6. The Cross was not essential. God had a different ideal in mind for mankind, found in Eden.
7. God makes covenants he can't necessarily keep.
8. Since "Jesus 1.0" failed to achieve "Plan A", R.M.'s sect awaits a "Jesus 2.0" to finish the job and set up an earthly kingdom; for them the heavenly kingdom is insufficient

The devotionals are intended to counter the above list. They contain evidence to empower Christians when engaged in apologetics with unbelievers. By making use of the topical index, they efficiently address questions as to who Jesus is and why He matters. It is my hope that every reader will be drawn into a deeper relationship with Jesus.

Process

When Roger Clevenger joined me in the studies with R.M., there were many times I had hope that R.M. was beginning to see the real Jesus. But, time and again, he'd ignore the passages we were studying. He wouldn't disparage them but he wouldn't comment on them, R.M. would change the subject. He wouldn't respond to the questions we put to him about the passages we read. Instead, he'd return to phrases he'd practiced and shared over and over again.

In my frustration, I decided to put together some very short passages and a message to R.M. So, I sent R.M. one of these each day from October 31, 2022 to March 23, 2023. My hope was that these might shake him out of his pattern of thinking. It definitely shook me up.

Why 144?

I started writing, not realizing how much work it would be. Most of the time they were very easy to write because God's word is so rich and because I was so familiar with R.M.'s needs. I didn't know when I was going to quit. Eventually I settled on 144 for two reasons. First, I thought the quantity of letters would be large enough that R.M. might take notice. Secondly, I had reached a point where I had compiled a pretty good overview of these topics, enough to be of value to others as well. Also, I must admit that I find the number 144 to be aesthetically pleasing.

The Meaning of the Tag Line

Each devotional ends with the same tag line, *"What is the Sword of the Spirit saying to we who have ears?"* This is not just directed at R.M. I, too, am the target along with every reader. In the end, it's not my words that have significance, it's the words of the Spirit. All readers can benefit from this mindset when studying scripture.

This tag line was constructed by splicing together a description of the Holy Scriptures from one of the Apostle Paul's letters along with a saying which Jesus used on a couple of occasions.

> "And the sword of the Spirit, which is the word of God." (Ephesians 6:17)

> "He who has ears to hear, let him hear." (Matthew 11:15)

It reminds the reader to personally and seriously reflect on the verses.

Useful for Years to Come

When you are finished reading this, it is my hope that you will continue to pick it up as a reference work. When you are teaching others, they will have questions about Jesus. They will ask about Jesus's deity (for example). Sometimes, your favorite verse on that subject might not satisfy the questioner. You can save time in research by having ready access to many of the other passages indicating Jesus's deity. This book provides that ready access with two extensive indices. The topical index has major categories covering the 8 aspects of Jesus's person and work mentioned earlier. Those categories are further broken down into 37 subcategories to speed your search for just the right verse to address the question.

 1
Jesus Predicts His Death and Resurrection

Luke 18:31–34 (NIV)

³¹Jesus took the Twelve aside and told them, "We are going up to Jerusalem, and everything that is written by the prophets about the Son of Man will be fulfilled. ³²He will be delivered over to the Gentiles. They will mock him, insult him and spit on him; ³³they will flog him and kill him. On the third day he will rise again."

³⁴The disciples did not understand any of this. Its meaning was hidden from them, and they did not know what he was talking about.

Knowing His disciples did not understand, Jesus was preparing them. This prediction of his death and resurrection would help them understand. Jesus didn't expect them to comprehend it in one telling; that's why he would explain this in more detail, many times, to ready them.

They needed to understand because they were going to be sharing the good news of his death and resurrection to the world.

What is the Sword of the Spirit saying to we who have ears?

2
Jesus Sets Peter Straight

Mark 8:31–33

³¹He then began to teach them that the Son of Man must suffer many things and be rejected by the elders, the chief priests and the teachers of the law, and that he must be killed and after three days rise again. ³²He spoke plainly about this, and Peter took him aside and began to rebuke him.

³³But when Jesus turned and looked at his disciples, he rebuked Peter. "Get behind me, Satan!" he said. "You do not have in mind the concerns of God, but merely human concerns."

Peter's words were Satanic because they defied God's will. Peter opposed the most glorious miracle of all eternity: Jesus' death on the cross.

Jesus' death is a miracle since only a holy and supernatural being could pay for the sins of mankind.

Jesus' death is glorious since his personal offering is worthy of our praise for eternity.

What is the Sword of the Spirit saying to we who have ears?

3
Two Blood Covenants: Only One Is Still in Effect

Exodus 24:8 (NIV)

Moses then took the blood, sprinkled it on the people and said, "This is the blood of the covenant that the Lord has made with you in accordance with all these words."

Luke 22:20 (NIV)

In the same way, after the supper he took the cup, saying, "This cup is the new covenant in my blood, which is poured out for you.

Hebrews 13:20–21 (NIV)

[20]Now may the God of peace, who through the blood of the eternal covenant brought back from the dead our Lord Jesus, that great Shepherd of the sheep, [21]equip you with everything good for doing his will, and may he work in us what is pleasing to him, through Jesus Christ, to whom be glory for ever and ever. Amen.

The LORD initiated a covenant with Israel with the blood of animals. Jesus established the New Covenant in his own blood.

Through Jesus' blood, God made the New Covenant last for eternity. There will be no other.

What is the Sword of the Spirit saying to we who have ears?

❦ 4 ❦
Angels Remind Wondering Women of the Plan

Luke 24:1–8 (NIV)

¹On the first day of the week, very early in the morning, the women took the spices they had prepared and went to the tomb. ²They found the stone rolled away from the tomb, ³but when they entered, they did not find the body of the Lord Jesus. ⁴While they were wondering about this, suddenly two men in clothes that gleamed like lightning stood beside them. ⁵In their fright the women bowed down with their faces to the ground, but the men said to them, "Why do you look for the living among the dead? ⁶He is not here; he has risen! Remember how he told you, while he was still with you in Galilee: ⁷'The Son of Man must be delivered over to the hands of sinners, be crucified and on the third day be raised again.' " ⁸Then they remembered his words.

Jesus' body was missing. The women wondered because they had forgotten the words of Jesus. The angels knew what the women needed—to remember what Jesus had said.

This was not a tragedy, but the fulfillment of Jesus' mission.

What is the Sword of the Spirit saying to we who have ears?

5
Cleopas & Friend Were Downcast, Not Believing All That The Prophets Had Spoken

Luke 24:13–27 (NIV)

¹³Now that same day two of them were going to a village called Emmaus, about seven miles a from Jerusalem. ¹⁴They were talking with each other about everything that had happened. ¹⁵As they talked and discussed these things with each other, Jesus himself came up and walked along with them; ¹⁶but they were kept from recognizing him.

¹⁷He asked them, "What are you discussing together as you walk along?"

They stood still, their faces downcast. ¹⁸One of them, named Cleopas, asked him, "Are you the only one visiting Jerusalem who does not know the things that have happened there in these days?"

¹⁹"What things?" he asked.

"About Jesus of Nazareth," they replied. "He was a prophet, powerful in word and deed before God and all the people. ²⁰The chief priests and our rulers handed him over to be sentenced to death, and they crucified him; ²¹but we had hoped that he was the one who was going to redeem Israel. And what is more, it is the third day since all this took place. ²²In addition, some of our women amazed us. They went to the tomb early this morning ²³but didn't find his body. They came and told us that they had seen a vision of angels, who said he was alive. ²⁴Then some of our companions went to the tomb and found it just as the women had said, but they did not see Jesus."

²⁵He said to them, "How foolish you are, and how slow to believe all that the prophets have spoken! ²⁶Did not the Messiah have to suffer these things and then enter his glory?" ²⁷And beginning with Moses and all the Prophets, he explained to them what was said in all the Scriptures concerning himself.

Cleopas and his friend were sad, they were still in mourning for Jesus. The reports of Jesus being alive caused them confusion. It did not make sense until Jesus pointed out all that the scriptures had foretold about him.

Jesus fulfilling the prophecies in scripture is not the same as acting out some script for a play. The scriptures proclaim God's loving intentions for mankind, Jesus fulfills them.

What is the Sword of the Spirit saying to we who have ears?

6
Jesus Eats Fish in the Flesh

Luke 24:36–44 (NIV)

^{36}While they were still talking about this, Jesus himself stood among them and said to them, "Peace be with you."

^{37}They were startled and frightened, thinking they saw a ghost. ^{38}He said to them, "Why are you troubled, and why do doubts rise in your minds? ^{39}Look at my hands and my feet. It is I myself! Touch me and see; a ghost does not have flesh and bones, as you see I have."

^{40}When he had said this, he showed them his hands and feet. ^{41}And while they still did not believe it because of joy and amazement, he asked them, "Do you have anything here to eat?" ^{42}They gave him a piece of broiled fish, ^{43}and he took it and ate it in their presence.

^{44}He said to them, "This is what I told you while I was still with you: Everything must be fulfilled that is written about me in the Law of Moses, the Prophets and the Psalms."

The disciples would not have been quite so startled if Jesus had merely appeared as a ghost. But Jesus was back in both spirit and in the flesh. This is the same flesh they had seen hanging on the cross.

Now, here he is, right in front of them. They are not just seeing him. They are touching him and seeing him eat fish. This is solid proof of his complete resurrection.

What is the Sword of the Spirit saying to we who have ears?

7
Closed Minds Couldn't Comprehend Passages About the Cross

Luke 24:45–47 (NIV)

⁴⁵Then he opened their minds so they could understand the Scriptures. ⁴⁶He told them, "This is what is written: The Messiah will suffer and rise from the dead on the third day, ⁴⁷and repentance for the forgiveness of sins will be preached in his name to all nations, beginning at Jerusalem.

At Jesus' resurrection, the disciples had felt a combination of shock, wonderment, and joy. They needed to move to a point of understanding the point of it all.

Prior to the crucifixion, Jesus had warned them these events must come to pass. The disciples didn't want to believe. On one occasion, when Jesus was predicting his suffering at the hands of their religious leaders, his death, and resurrection, Peter openly rebuked Jesus (Matthew 16:21–27). Peter couldn't bear to think of such things happening to the one he put his hopes in. And Peter wasn't the only one who didn't understand.

After the resurrection, it was time for Jesus to open their minds to fully understand the purpose of his sufferings. Jesus returned to the Scriptures predicting these things. Now, with the resurrected Jesus explaining, the disciples could comprehend them.

The disciples went on to preach with authority, preaching "in his name," Jesus the Messiah. They preached that people should confess their sins and repent. And they preached the good news that repentance and baptism would result in forgiveness (Acts 2:38). They were able to preach because they understood.

What is the Sword of the Spirit saying to we who have ears?

8
The Kindest Cut of All Is God's Plan

Acts 2:22-23 (NIV)

²²"Fellow Israelites, listen to this: Jesus of Nazareth was a man accredited by God to you by miracles, wonders and signs, which God did among you through him, as you yourselves know. ²³This man was handed over to you by God's deliberate plan and foreknowledge; and you, with the help of wicked men, put him to death by nailing him to the cross."

Acts 2:29-31 (NIV)

²⁹"Fellow Israelites, I can tell you confidently that the patriarch David died and was buried, and his tomb is here to this day. ³⁰But he was a prophet and knew that God had promised him on oath that he would place one of his descendants on his throne. ³¹Seeing what was to come, he spoke of the resurrection of the Messiah, that he was not abandoned to the realm of the dead, nor did his body see decay."

Acts 2:36-37 (NIV)

³⁶"Therefore let all Israel be assured of this: God has made this Jesus, whom you crucified, both Lord and Messiah."

³⁷When the people heard this, they were cut to the heart and said to Peter and the other apostles, "Brothers, what shall we do?"

These excerpts are from Peter's message given 50 days after Jesus' resurrection. On that day, thousands heard about the Messiah's crucifixion and resurrection.

Why were they cut to the heart? These Jews had not personally nailed Jesus to the cross. They had not personally arrested Jesus; their religious leaders took care of that. Nor had they sentenced Him to death; the Romans did that. But there may have been a few were in the crowd calling for Jesus' crucifixion.

But they, like we, are sinners — sinners for whom Jesus died. That certainly cuts to the heart. Peter gave them the God-given answer* to their question, "What shall we do?" About 3,000 of them responded in the God-given way (Acts 2:41).

What is the Sword of the Spirit saying to we who have ears?

---

* The God-given answer to "what shall we do?" is found in Acts 2:38 — "And Peter said to them, 'repent and be baptized every one of you in the name of Jesus Christ for the forgiveness of your sins, and you will receive the gift of the Holy Spirit.'" There were about 3,000 who responded in faith — Acts 2:41, "So those who received his word were baptized and there were added that day about three thousand souls."

9
Peter Preaches Good News After a Lame Man Is Healed

Acts 3:6–7 (NIV)

[6]Then Peter said, "Silver or gold I do not have, but what I do have I give you. In the name of Jesus Christ of Nazareth, walk." [7]Taking him by the right hand, he helped him up, and instantly the man's feet and ankles became strong.

Acts 3:11–20 (NIV)

[11]While the man held on to Peter and John, all the people were astonished and came running to them in the place called Solomon's Colonnade. [12]When Peter saw this, he said to them: "Fellow Israelites, why does this surprise you? Why do you stare at us as if by our own power or godliness we had made this man walk? [13]The God of Abraham, Isaac and Jacob, the God of our fathers, has glorified his servant Jesus. You handed him over to be killed, and you disowned him before Pilate, though he had decided to let him go. [14]You disowned the Holy and Righteous One and asked that a murderer be released to you. [15]You killed the author of life, but God raised him from the dead. We are witnesses of this. [16]By faith in the name of Jesus, this man whom you see and know was made strong. It is Jesus' name and the faith that comes through him that has completely healed him, as you can all see.

[17]"Now, fellow Israelites, I know that you acted in ignorance, as did your leaders. [18]But this is how God fulfilled what he had foretold through all the prophets, saying that his Messiah would suffer. [19]Repent, then, and turn to God, so that your sins may be wiped out, that times of refreshing may come from the Lord, [20]and that he may send the Messiah, who has been appointed for you—even Jesus.

Peter explained who it was that provided the healing power for this lame man to be able to walk. It was Jesus, the author of life who enables all walking in the first place.

Their reaction? It is naturally quite terrifying to learn of your role in Jesus' death. Our sins are terrible, indeed.

Thankfully, his death is an essential part of God's plan. His death and resurrection make it possible for us to...

> "Repent, then, and turn to God, so that your sins may be wiped out, that times of refreshing may come from the Lord." (Acts 3:19)

What is the Sword of the Spirit saying to we who have ears?

10
Jesus Lays Out the Glorification Plan

John 12:28–33 (NIV)

[28]"Father, glorify your name!"

Then a voice came from heaven, "I have glorified it, and will glorify it again." [29]The crowd that was there and heard it said it had thundered; others said an angel had spoken to him.

[30]Jesus said, "This voice was for your benefit, not mine. [31]Now is the time for judgment on this world; now the prince of this world will be driven out. [32]And I, when I am lifted up from the earth, will draw all people to myself." [33]He said this to show the kind of death he was going to die.

The voice of the Father answered Jesus's prayer. For the benefit of those present, and our benefit, Jesus explained.

The Father has glorified His name many times; He glorified it in creation, through the flood, in the rescue of Lot and the destruction of Sodom, and by his liberation of Israel from the hand of Pharaoh. This is a small sampling of how the Father has previously glorified His name.

How will he "… glorify it again?" Jesus explains the glorification is through His death and all that He and the Father accomplish by the cross. God's power over death is proven in the resurrection. God's judgment is not voided, sin is fully paid for in the cross. Jesus draws all mankind to Himself, whether they like it or not. Those who believe join Jesus for eternity, those who do not will join Satan in hell.

Here are some other sayings of Jesus which shine a light on the glory of the Father's name and his own:
- John 17:26 "I made known to them your name"
- Matthew 28:18-20 "...make disciples of all nations, baptizing them in the name of the Father and of the Son and of the Holy Spirit"
- John 10:30 "I and the Father are one"
- John 11:25-26 "Jesus said to her, "I am the resurrection and the life. Whoever believes in me, though he die, yet shall he live, and everyone who
- lives and believes in me shall never die. Do you believe this?"

Here we learn how much glory that Jesus' name carries with it:

Philippians 2:9-11 (ESV)

9"Therefore God has highly exalted him and bestowed on him the name that is above every name, 10so that at the name of Jesus every knee should bow, in heaven and on earth and under the earth, 11and every tongue confess that Jesus Christ is Lord, to the glory of God the Father."

I suspect that "Jesus" is a family name shared by the Father and the Son. Perhaps it is also shared by the Holy Spirit.

What is the Sword of the Spirit saying to we who have ears?

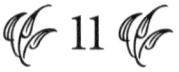
11
A Psalm Predicts Jesus' Resurrection

Acts 13:26–35 (NASB95)

²⁶Brethren, sons of Abraham's family, and those among you who fear God, to us the message of this salvation has been sent. ²⁷For those who live in Jerusalem, and their rulers, recognizing neither Him nor the utterances of the prophets which are read every Sabbath, fulfilled these by condemning Him. ²⁸And though they found no ground for [putting Him to] death, they asked Pilate that He be executed. ²⁹When they had carried out all that was written concerning Him, they took Him down from the cross and laid Him in a tomb. ³⁰But God raised Him from the dead; ³¹and for many days He appeared to those who came up with Him from Galilee to Jerusalem, the very ones who are now His witnesses to the people. ³²"And we preach to you the good news of the promise made to the fathers, ³³that God has fulfilled this promise to our children in that He raised up Jesus, as **it is also written in the second Psalm,**

'You are My Son; today I have begotten You.

³⁴As for the fact that He raised Him up from the dead, no longer to return to decay, He has spoken in this way:

"I will give you the holy and sure blessings of David."

³⁵Therefore He also says in another Psalm,

"You will not allow Your Holy One to undergo decay."

In this speech, Paul tells how the Father's raising of Jesus fulfills Psalm 2. Some English translations further obscure Paul's point* by rendering γεγέννηκά "become your Father" instead of "begotten You." But both approaches obscure how the prophecy at Psalm 2:7 is being fulfilled, to a greater or lesser degree.

---

* Reviewing the first 32 English translations of Acts 13:33 available at https://biblehub.com/acts/13-33.htm, we find that 17 render the Greek word γεγέννηκά (g1080) into the English "begotten," whereas fifteen render it "become your father." The Hebrew for begotten is יְלִדְתִּיךָ (h3205) translated into English variously as "to bear, bring forth, beget, gender, travail." Greek and Hebrew language information from www.blueletterbible.org on 11/29/2024.

The essence of that word is "to bring forth," an action which can apply to bringing forth from the grave as well as from the womb. Paul usage is clear; when God raised up Jesus, that act was the fulfillment of the promise from the 2nd Psalm, "today I have begotten you" (Acts 13:33).

The "TODAY" referenced is not a day in which the Father "adopted" Jesus as His Son, for Jesus has eternally been the Son of God. Nor is it the day Jesus was "brought forth" from the virgin Mary, about 33 years earlier. That "TODAY" is the day when the Father "brought forth" His Son from the grave.

What is the Sword of the Spirit saying to we who have ears?

❦ 12 ❦
Resurrection and Sacrifice Prophesies

Genesis 20:7 (NIV)

Now return the man's wife, for he is a prophet, and he will pray for you and you will live. But if you do not return her, you may be sure that you and all who belong to you will die."

God revealed to Abimilech (king of Gerar) that Abraham was His prophet. God would use the prophet Abraham to share an essential message.

Hebrews 11:17–19 (NIV)

By faith Abraham, when God tested him, offered Isaac as a sacrifice. He who had embraced the promises was about to sacrifice his one and only son, [18]even though God had said to him, "It is through Isaac that your offspring will be reckoned." [19]Abraham reasoned that God could even raise the dead, and so in a manner of speaking he did receive Isaac back from death.

God had made an important promise to Abraham about what he would accomplish through the descendants of Isaac. Abraham had faith in God's resurrection power, should that be needed to fulfill those promises.

Genesis 22:6–8 (NIV)

Abraham took the wood for the burnt offering and placed it on his son Isaac, and he himself carried the fire and the knife. As the two of them went on together, [7]Isaac spoke up and said to his father Abraham, "Father?"

"Yes, my son?" Abraham replied.

"The fire and wood are here," Isaac said, "but where is the lamb for the burnt offering?"

Abraham answered, "God himself will provide the lamb for the burnt offering, my son." And the two of them went on together.

Abraham prophesied that God would provide the lamb for the offering.

John 1:29 (NIV)

The next day John saw Jesus coming toward him and said, "Look, the Lamb of God, who takes away the sin of the world!

As Abraham prophesied, God provided the required sacrificial lamb. John the Baptist, another prophet of God, introduced Jesus as that Lamb of God.

What is the Sword of the Spirit saying to we who have ears?

13
Jesus Prayed in the Garden, What Was The Father's Answer?

Luke 22:41-42 (NIV)

He withdrew about a stone's throw beyond them, knelt down and prayed, "Father, if you are willing, take this cup from me; yet not my will, but yours be done."

Hebrews 5:7 (NIV)

During the days of Jesus's life on earth, he offered up prayers and petitions with fervent cries and tears to the one who could save him from death, and he was heard because of his reverent submission.

The Father heard the Son's prayer. The Father answered: it was his will that Jesus drink the cup of death. Jesus agreed, "not my will, but yours be done."

What is the Sword of the Spirit saying to we who have ears?

14
Glory: When Did Jesus First Have It?

John 17:5 (NIV)

"And now, Father, glorify me in your presence with the glory I had with you before the world began."

What's the big deal about "glory?" Glory is being worthy of praise and honor, it's about being an authentic "big deal."

Jesus has had glory a long time ago. But he's not just older than the world; Jesus is eternal. "Jesus Christ is the same yesterday and today and forever" (Hebrews 13:8).

God the Father has been glorifying the Son forever. That's the most significant glory of all.

What is the Sword of the Spirit saying to we who have ears?

15
Unwitting Sinners Follow God's Plan

Acts 13:27–28 (NIV)

The people of Jerusalem and their rulers did not recognize Jesus, yet in condemning him they fulfilled the words of the prophets that are read every Sabbath. 28 Though they found no proper grounds for a death sentence, they asked Pilate to have him executed.

Among the Jewish rulers who sentenced Jesus to death, some knowingly sinned. Yet, in the very same act of sentencing Jesus to death, they unknowingly participated in the fulfilment of the promises of God through the prophets.

What is the Sword of the Spirit saying to we who have ears?

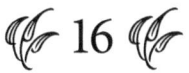 16
The Disciples Have a Hard Time Listening to Jesus, in Spite of the Transfiguration

Mark 9:7–10 (NIV)

⁷Then a cloud appeared and covered them, and a voice came from the cloud: **"This is my Son, whom I love. Listen to him!"**

⁸Suddenly, when they looked around, they no longer saw anyone with them except Jesus.

⁹As they were coming down the mountain, Jesus gave them orders not to tell anyone what they had seen until the Son of Man had risen from the dead. ¹⁰They kept the matter to themselves, discussing what "rising from the dead" meant.

Prior to the events on the Mount of Transfiguration, Jesus had revealed his upcoming death and resurrection (Mark 8:29–33). On the mount, the disciples hear the Father's voice tell the disciples to listen to Jesus.

Again, Jesus predicts His own death and resurrection. The disciples do not appear to be listening with understanding.

What is the Sword of the Spirit saying to we who have ears?

17
Herod, Pilate, *et al*, Doing As God's Power and Will Had Foreordained

Acts 4:23–31 (NIV)

²³On their release, Peter and John went back to their own people and reported all that the chief priests and the elders had said to them. ²⁴When they heard this, they raised their voices together in prayer to God. "Sovereign Lord," they said, "you made the heavens and the earth and the sea, and everything in them. ²⁵You spoke by the Holy Spirit through the mouth of your servant, our father David:

> "'Why do the nations rage and the peoples plot in vain?
> ²⁶The kings of the earth rise up and the rulers band together against the Lord and against his anointed one.'
> [*From Psalm 2:1–2*]

²⁷Indeed Herod and Pontius Pilate met together with the Gentiles and the people of Israel in this city to conspire against your holy servant Jesus, whom you anointed. ²⁸They did what your power and will had decided beforehand should happen. ²⁹Now, Lord, consider their threats and enable your servants to speak your word with great boldness. ³⁰Stretch out your hand to heal and perform signs and wonders through the name of your holy servant Jesus."

³¹After they prayed, the place where they were meeting was shaken. And they were all filled with the Holy Spirit and spoke the word of God boldly.

In this prayer, Peter and John praise what God was doing through them: speaking the word with boldness and performing miraculous signs. God was doing these great things through two repentant sinners.

But God does not merely work through repentant sinners. Unrepentant Herod and Pontious Pilate (and so many others) had sinned directly against Jesus. But God Almighty worked out His will through these even in the midst of their sins. They were fighting God's will, yet God worked His will through them just the same.

This was not just the perspective of the apostles Peter and John. The apostle Paul would also teach how God had used the sinful actions of men to fulfill His preordained will (Acts 13:27-28). This consistency of message is what we should expect, since the apostles are filled with the Holy Spirit.

What is the Sword of the Spirit saying to we who have ears?

 18

The Ethiopian Treasurer Gets Good News

Acts 8:26–38 (NIV)

²⁶Now an angel of the Lord said to Philip, "Go south to the road—the desert road—that goes down from Jerusalem to Gaza." ²⁷So he started out, and on his way he met an Ethiopian eunuch, an important official in charge of all the treasury of the Kandake (which means "queen of the Ethiopians"). This man had gone to Jerusalem to worship, ²⁸and on his way home was sitting in his chariot reading the Book of Isaiah the prophet. ²⁹The Spirit told Philip, "Go to that chariot and stay near it."

³⁰Then Philip ran up to the chariot and heard the man reading Isaiah the prophet. "Do you understand what you are reading?" Philip asked.

³¹"How can I," he said, "unless someone explains it to me?" So he invited Philip to come up and sit with him.

³²This is the passage of Scripture the eunuch was reading:

> "He was led like a sheep to the slaughter,
> and as a lamb before its shearer is silent,
> so he did not open his mouth.
> ³³In his humiliation he was deprived of justice.
> Who can speak of his descendants?
> For his life was taken from the earth." [Isaiah 53:7–8]

³⁴The eunuch asked Philip, "Tell me, please, who is the prophet talking about, himself or someone else?" ³⁵Then Philip began with that very passage of Scripture and told him the good news about Jesus.

³⁶As they traveled along the road, they came to some water and the eunuch said, "Look, here is water. What can stand in the way of my being baptized?" ³⁸And he gave orders to stop the chariot. Then both Philip and the eunuch went down into the water and Philip baptized him. ³⁹When they came up out of the water, the Spirit of the Lord suddenly took Philip away, and the eunuch did not see him again, but went on his way rejoicing.

The silent lamb that was led to the slaughter was Jesus. This passage from Isaiah describes how he did not defend himself before Pilate. One has to ask, "How could this be described as good news, when Jesus received injustice?" Is it good news that Jesus did not put up a fight?

Yet Philip shared the news. As a result, the Ethiopian was baptized and went on his way rejoicing. So it must have been good news, but why?

It is very good news because Jesus laid down his life as a sacrifice for his sins. It's good news that Jesus took up his life again. That's what caused the Ethiopian's rejoicing; he had just received forgiveness and new life in Jesus.

What is the Sword of the Spirit saying to we who have ears?

19
The First Thing You Need to Know About the Messiah

Mark 8:29–33 (NIV)

"But what about you?" he asked. "Who do you say I am?"

Peter answered, **"You are the Messiah."**

³⁰Jesus warned them not to tell anyone about him.

³¹He then began to teach them that the Son of Man must suffer many things and be rejected by the elders, the chief priests and the teachers of the law, and that he must be killed and after three days rise again. ³²He spoke plainly about this, and Peter took him aside and began to rebuke him.

³³But when Jesus turned and looked at his disciples, he rebuked Peter. "Get behind me, Satan!" he said. "You do not have in mind the concerns of God, but merely human concerns."

Jesus is the Messiah. Now days, all kinds of people are declared to be a messiah or writers of messianic literature.

At the time Peter declared it, the title messiah had a very specific meaning. A messiah was an "anointed one." God had the Jews anoint people with oil when they took the offices of judge, prophet, priest, and king.

In fact, Jesus was the Messiah in all four ways. But Peter seems to have understood Jesus as being that long anticipated King above all kings.

The Messiah is the Christ, the King.* Peter declared it. Jesus' affirmed it. But Jesus asked him to keep it quiet about it, for the time being.

Then Jesus rocks Peter's world. Peter is not ready to have a Messiah that will be killed by His own people.

Point #1 of being the Messiah is His mission — death on the cross. To reject the Messiah's mission is to deny His authority. If you reject His mission then you reject Him, you reject God, and you align yourself with Satan.

Like Peter, we must submit to King Jesus on His terms. That's the way to align our concerns with God's. We cannot settle for a King who did not willingly go to the cross.

What is the Sword of the Spirit saying to we who have ears?

---

* "Christ" is the Greek for the Hebrew "Messiah." The "Messiah" as king is a usage easily confirmed by these two passages: Mark 15:32, "Let his Messiah, this king of Israel, come down now from the cross...", and Luke 23:2, "...He opposes payment of taxes to Caesar and claims to be Messiah, a king".

20
A Retreat Alone with the Disciples

Mark 9:30–32 (NIV)

³⁰They left that place and passed through Galilee. Jesus did not want anyone to know where they were, ³¹because he was teaching his disciples. He said to them, "The Son of Man is going to be delivered into the hands of men. They will kill him, and after three days he will rise." ³²But they did not understand what he meant and were afraid to ask him about it.

The disciples received, yet again, Jesus' teaching on his death, burial, and resurrection. This time Jesus arranged it away from the crowds. When fear blocks learning, things are hard to understand. When fear blocks learning, things are hard to understand. Jesus understood this, so He told them several times what the plan was.

What is the Sword of the Spirit saying to we who have ears?

21
This Time, the Disciples Are Even More Afraid

Mark 10:32–34 (NIV)

³²They were on their way up to Jerusalem, with Jesus leading the way, and the disciples were astonished, while those who followed were afraid. Again he took the Twelve aside and told them what was going to happen to him. ³³"We are going up to Jerusalem," he said, "and the Son of Man will be delivered over to the chief priests and the teachers of the law. They will condemn him to death and will hand him over to the Gentiles, ³⁴who will mock him and spit on him, flog him and kill him. Three days later he will rise."

The last time Jesus taught this subject (Mark 9:30–32), the disciples were afraid to question Him about it. Now they are shocked to see Jesus leading them to the town where His mortal enemies have power. Jesus had been revealing his plan quite plainly. But the disciples has been hoping Jesus was speaking in symbols, ab out something less serious -- much less serious than the sins of the whole world.

What is the Sword of the Spirit saying to we who have ears?

22
A Parable in Which Jesus Predicts His Passing and the Parties Involved

Mark 12:1–12 (NIV)

¹Jesus then began to speak to them in parables: "A man planted a vineyard. He put a wall around it, dug a pit for the winepress and built a watchtower. Then he rented the vineyard to some farmers and moved to another place. ²At harvest time he sent a servant to the tenants to collect from them some of the fruit of the vineyard. ³But they seized him, beat him and sent him away empty-handed. ⁴Then he sent another servant to them; they struck this man on the head and treated him shamefully. ⁵He sent still another, and that one they killed. He sent many others; some of them they beat, others they killed.

⁶"He had one left to send, a son, whom he loved. He sent him last of all, saying, 'They will respect my son.'

⁷"But the tenants said to one another, 'This is the heir. Come, let's kill him, and the inheritance will be ours.' ⁸So they took him and killed him, and threw him out of the vineyard.

⁹"What then will the owner of the vineyard do? He will come and kill those tenants and give the vineyard to others. ¹⁰Haven't you read this passage of Scripture:

> "'The stone the builders rejected has become the cornerstone;
> ¹¹**the Lord has done this, and it is marvelous in our eyes**'"
> [*Psalm 118:22-23*]

¹²Then the chief priests, the teachers of the law and the elders looked for a way to arrest him because they knew he had spoken the parable against them. But they were afraid of the crowd; so they left him and went away.

After all is said and done, who is responsible for Jesus' death? It was God Himself who had this planned all along! "The stone the builders rejected has become the cornerstone; the Lord has done this, and it is marvelous in our eyes." In love of the world, the Lord sent his only begotten son into the world knowing that he would be rejected.

Let it also be marvelous in our eyes. Let our eyes open up to see His love.

What is the Sword of the Spirit saying to we who have ears?

23
Mary Names Him "Jesus" and Much Is Fulfilled

Matthew 1:20–23 (NIV)

[20]But after he had considered this, an angel of the Lord appeared to him in a dream and said, "Joseph son of David, do not be afraid to take Mary home as your wife, because what is conceived in her is from the Holy Spirit. [21]She will give birth to a son, and you are to give him the name Jesus[*], because he will save his people from their sins."

[22]**All this took place to fulfill what the Lord had said** through the prophet: [23]"The virgin will conceive and give birth to a son, and they will call him Immanuel" (which means "God with us").

---

[*] Jesus (Iesous) is the Greek equivalent of the Hebrew "Joshua" (yehoshua`), meaning "Yahweh is salvation," per https://www.internationalstandardbible.com/J/jesus-christ-2.html. The original name of Joshua was Hoshea (הוֹשֵׁעַ, H1954, saving), as appears in Numbers 13:8,16, which was changed by Moses into Jehoshua (יְהוֹשֻׁעַ, H3091, Jehovah is his salvation), per https://www.biblicalcyclopedia.com/J/jesus-christ.html.

Matthew identified a prophecy about Jesus from Isaiah 7:14. Jesus' name defines his person and his mission: "Yahweh is salvation". Yahweh is the name the Jews received for God.

It is also right to call Jesus "Immanuel." Though Yahweh has saved in the past and continues to save, He is *now* saving by being "with us" as God come in the flesh.

What is the Sword of the Spirit saying to we who have ears?

24
Abraham Trusted Wisely

Mark 12:22–27 (NIV)

[Sadducess speaking in cynical fashion] ²²In fact, none of the seven left any children. Last of all, the woman died too. ²³At the resurrection whose wife will she be, since the seven were married to her?"

²⁴Jesus replied, "**Are you not in error because you do not know the Scriptures or the power of God?** ²⁵When the dead rise, they will neither marry nor be given in marriage; they will be like the angels in heaven. ²⁶Now about the dead rising—have you not read in the Book of Moses, in the account of the burning bush, how God said to him, '**I am the God of Abraham**, the God of Isaac, and the God of Jacob'? ²⁷**He is not the God of the dead, but of the living**. You are badly mistaken!"

Abraham trusted in God and moved away from the land of his birth to places which God directed him. All the promises God made to Abraham were not fulfilled during Abraham's lifetime. Yet God is still Abraham's God, Abraham is living still.

Nonetheless, we know that God did not make these promises in vain. Jesus shows us that they have been fulfilled when He conveys to His disciples an episode from Abraham's time in the afterlife.

Luke 16:27-31 (NIV)

[*Rich Man in torment speaking*] ²⁷"He answered,
'Then I beg you, father, send Lazarus to my family, ²⁸for I have five brothers. Let him warn them, so that they will not also come to this place of torment.'

²⁹"Abraham replied, 'They have Moses and the Prophets; let them listen to them.'

³⁰"'No, father Abraham,' he said, 'but if someone from the dead goes to them, they will repent.'

³¹"He said to him, '**If they do not listen to Moses and the Prophets, they will not be convinced even if someone rises from the dead.**'"

Lazarus had been sent to a place of blessing, a place at Abraham's side. The "I AM," is still Abraham's God, and continues to fulfill His promises.

What is the Sword of the Spirit saying to we who have ears?

25
Judas and the Eleven Are Reminded That Scripture Must Be Fulfilled

Mark 14:17–21 (NIV)

¹⁷When evening came, Jesus arrived with the Twelve. ¹⁸While they were reclining at the table eating, he said, "Truly I tell you, one of you will betray me—one who is eating with me."

¹⁹They were saddened, and one by one they said to him, "Surely you don't mean me?"

²⁰"It is one of the Twelve," he replied, "one who dips bread into the bowl with me. ²¹**The Son of Man will go just as it is written about him.** But woe to that man who betrays the Son of Man! It would be better for him if he had not been born."

Jesus' betrayal by Judas was predicted in the 41st Psalm. He is referencing that Psalm when He says, "The Son of Man will go just as it is written about him." Jesus is not planning on going any way other than the scriptural way.

Psalm 41:9 (NIV)

Even my close friend,
someone I trusted,
one who shared my bread,
has turned against me.

The way promised in scripture is the way of the cross.

What is the Sword of the Spirit saying to we who have ears?

26
Prophets' Prophecies of Savior's Sufferings Serve the Saints

1 Peter 1:10–12 (NIV)

¹⁰Concerning this salvation, the prophets, who spoke of the grace that was to come to you, searched intently and with the greatest care, ¹¹trying to find out the time and circumstances to which the Spirit of Christ in them was pointing when he predicted the sufferings of the Messiah and the glories that would follow. ¹²It was revealed to them that they were not serving themselves but you, when they spoke of the things that have now been told you by those who have preached the gospel to you by the Holy Spirit sent from heaven. Even angels long to look into these things.

Curious prophets tried to uncover the time of the Savior's sufferings; angels also wanted to know. But the Holy Spirit intended that these prophecies of suffering would serve the Christians receiving this letter (1 Peter) long after those prophets had died.

So, who told these ancient prophets what to write?

The answer can be found in 1 Peter 1:11, "...the Spirit of Christ in them... he predicted the sufferings of the Messiah..." It was Christ Himself who predicted his own sufferings and glory.

What is the Sword of the Spirit saying to we who have ears?

27
Jesus Tells the Purpose of His Upcoming Death

Mark 14:22–26 (NIV)

²²While they were eating, Jesus took bread, and when he had given thanks, he broke it and gave it to his disciples, saying, "Take it; this is my body."

²³Then he took a cup, and when he had given thanks, he gave it to them, and they all drank from it.

²⁴"This is my blood of the covenant, which is poured out for many," he said to them. ²⁵"Truly I tell you, I will not drink again from the fruit of the vine until that day when I drink it new in the kingdom of God."

²⁶When they had sung a hymn, they went out to the Mount of Olives.

Jesus is making a covenant which requires blood. The blood required is His blood. He poured it out for the benefit of many. In Hebrews 9:15–28, the Holy Spirit provides a detailed explanation for the necessity of blood.

As we reconsider Jesus' words at the last supper, we can know more fully that *There was One who was willing to die in my stead, That a soul so unworthy might live.**

What is the Sword of the Spirit saying to we who have ears?

---

* This is the first line of the first verse in the hymn "Nailed to the Cross" by Carrie Ellis Breck (1899).

28
Jesus Tells His Unrighteous Judge How Judgment Day Will Be Handled

Mark 14:61–64 (NIV)

⁶¹But Jesus remained silent and gave no answer.

Again the high priest asked him, "Are you the Messiah, the Son of the Blessed One?"

⁶²"I am," said Jesus. "And you will see the Son of Man sitting at the right hand of the Mighty One and coming on the clouds of heaven."

⁶³The high priest tore his clothes. "Why do we need any more witnesses?" he asked. ⁶⁴"You have heard the blasphemy. What do you think?"

Being *at the right hand of the Mighty One and coming on the clouds of heaven* indicates that Jesus will be doing the judging, come judgment day Based on the high priests familiarity with the book of Daniel, he correctly understood that Jesus claimed to be the "Son of Man" described in Daniel 7:13-14. Tragically, he did not believe Jesus' claim to deity.

Jesus used similar language when he lays out in more detail his pivotal role in the final judgment.

Matthew 24:30–31 (NIV)

[30]"Then will appear the sign of the Son of Man in heaven. And then all the peoples of the earth will mourn when they see the Son of Man coming on the clouds of heaven, with power and great glory. [31]And he will send his angels with a loud trumpet call, and they will gather his elect from the four winds, from one end of the heavens to the other.

One wonders if that unrighteous judge of Jesus, the high priest Caiaphas, will end up being among those mourning at the coming of the Son of Man, rather than among his gathered elect.

What is the Sword of the Spirit saying to we who have ears?

29
"Coming into the World," a Unique Event

Hebrews 10:5–10 (NIV)

⁵Therefore, when Christ came into the world, he said:

> "Sacrifice and offering you did not desire,
> but a body you prepared for me;
> ⁶with burnt offerings and sin offerings
> you were not pleased.
>
> ⁷Then I said, 'Here I am—it is written about me in the scroll—
> I have come to do your will, my God.'" *[from Psalm 40:6-8]*

⁸First he said, "Sacrifices and offerings, burnt offerings and sin offerings you did not desire, nor were you pleased with them"—though they were offered in accordance with the law. ⁹Then he said, "Here I am, I have come to do your will." He sets aside the first to establish the second. ¹⁰And by that will, we have been made holy through the sacrifice of the body of Jesus Christ once for all.

Only one has entered into humanity with His own plan for His life, Jesus. And Jesus did not come to do the 3rd will of God, nor did He come to do the 2nd will of God. Jesus came to do God's will, all of it.

What is the Sword of the Spirit saying to we who have ears?

30
There's Purpose in Christ's Death and Return to Life

Romans 14:8–9 (NIV)

⁸If we live, we live for the Lord; and if we die, we die for the Lord. So, whether we live or die, we belong to the Lord. ⁹For this very reason, Christ died and returned to life so that he might be the Lord of both the dead and the living.

Some call the death of Jesus a tragic shame. I have heard more than a few say that Jesus' death did not accomplish much. Many of both camps think either that His death should not have happened at all or happened in some other way.

From this passage, we've learned the purpose of Jesus' death and resurrection: that He might be the Lord of the dead and the living

What is the Sword of the Spirit saying to we who have ears?

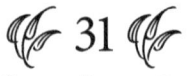 31
Responsibility for the Greatest Sacrifice

Hebrews 7:25–28 (NIV)

²⁵Therefore he is able to save completely those who come to God through him, because he always lives to intercede for them.

²⁶Such a high priest truly meets our need—one who is holy, blameless, pure, set apart from sinners, exalted above the heavens. ²⁷Unlike the other high priests, he does not need to offer sacrifices day after day, first for his own sins, and then for the sins of the people. *He sacrificed* for their sins once for all *when he offered himself.* ²⁸For the law appoints as high priests men in all their weakness; but the oath, which came after the law, appointed the Son, who has been made perfect forever.

Jesus was the sacrifice for sins. Who was it that made this offering?

Abraham and the Levitical priests offered lambs, bulls, and goats. Many people consider self-sacrifice greater. Jesus, being both the greatest high priest of all time as well as the greatest of all time, is in a unique position to offer the greatest self-sacrifice of all time.

What is the Sword of the Spirit saying to we who have ears?

32
Jesus Spells Out His Total Command of the Situation

John 10:17–18 (NIV)

¹⁷The reason my Father loves me is that I lay down my life—only to take it up again. ¹⁸No one takes it from me, but I lay it down of my own accord. I have authority to lay it down and authority to take it up again. This command I received from my Father."

Jesus, who could have called 12 legions of angels (Matthew 26:53), was never in danger of having his life taken from Him.

What is the Sword of the Spirit saying to we who have ears?

33
Who Resurrected Jesus?

John 2:18–22 (NIV)

¹⁸The Jews then responded to him, "What sign can you show us to prove your authority to do all this?"

¹⁹Jesus answered them, "Destroy this temple, and I will raise it again in three days."

²⁰They replied, "It has taken 46 years to build this temple, and you are going to raise it in 3 days?" ²¹But the temple he had spoken of was his body. ²²After he was raised from the dead, his disciples recalled what he had said. Then they believed the scripture and the words that Jesus had spoken.

The Jews asked for a sign of Jesus' authority. Jesus provides the ultimate sign: He suggests that they kill him, after which He will perform his own resurrection.

To top it off, this scenario had already been predicted by scripture (*They* [the disciples] *believed the scripture and the words that Jesus had spoken.*). For a specific scripture dramatically predicting Jesus's death and resurrection, I generally recommend Isaiah 53. In this passage, the crucifixion and resurrection are readily seen by those with a basic familiarity with the events of Jesus's life.

What is the Sword of the Spirit saying to we who have ears?

34
Unique Arrival from Up Above

John 3:13, 31 (NIV)

¹³No one has ever gone into heaven except the one who came from heaven—the Son of Man. ... ³¹The one who comes **from above is above all**; the one who is from the earth belongs to the earth, and speaks as one from the earth. The one who comes **from heaven is above all**.

Never before, nor since, has one come from heaven to earth to become flesh. That's Jesus, who ascended back into heaven after His resurrection from the dead. He is above all.

What is the Sword of the Spirit saying to we who have ears?

35
The Measuring Rod of God's Love

John 3:16 (NIV)

For God so loved the world that he gave **his one and only Son**, that whoever believes in him shall not perish but have eternal life.

When a child begins to think about parental love, she might wonder how much love she receives in relation to her siblings. Humans lack the ability to measure even such a common love. But the measure of God's love is certain; it is the giving of His one-and-only Son. We are loved.

What is the Sword of the Spirit saying to we who have ears?

36
Who Has the Whole World in His Hands?

John 3:35–36 (NIV)

³⁵The Father loves the Son and has placed everything in his hands. ³⁶Whoever believes in the Son has eternal life, but whoever rejects the Son will not see life, for God's wrath remains on them.

A song I sang in childhood has the title "He's Got the Whole World in His Hands." The song does not identify "He." But The Holy Spirit, speaking through John The Baptist, testifies that it is Jesus who has the whole world in his hands (John 3:35).

What is the Sword of the Spirit saying to we who have ears?

37
Jesus Calls Us to Himself

John 15:5 (NIV)

"I am the vine; you are the branches. If you remain in me and I in you, you will bear much fruit; apart from me you can do nothing.

Jesus, the vine and divine, makes His offer. Awaiting a "better" offer from another "Jesus" would be disastrous.

What is the Sword of the Spirit saying to we who have ears?

38
God Swears

Hebrews 7:20–24 (NIV)

[20]And it was not without an oath! Others became priests without any oath, [21]but he became a priest with an oath when God said to him:

> "The Lord has sworn
> and will not change his mind:
> 'You are a priest forever.' " *[Psalm 110:4]*

[22]Because of this oath, Jesus has become the guarantor of a better covenant.

[23]Now there have been many of those priests, since death prevented them from continuing in office; [24]but because Jesus lives forever, he has a permanent priesthood.

According to sworn covenant, God declared Jesus to be an eternal priest. Eternal includes today! What about tomorrow? Jesus will be priest tomorrow because God will not change His mind (Hebrews 7:21), He'll not go back on his oath.

What is the Sword of the Spirit saying to we who have ears?

39
A New Covenant Was Planned, Long, Long Ago

Hebrews 8:8–13 (NIV)

⁸For finding fault with them, he said,

> "The days are coming, declares the Lord,
>   when I will make a new covenant
> with the people of Israel
>   and with the people of Judah.
>
> ⁹It will not be like the covenant
>   I made with their ancestors
> when I took them by the hand
>   to lead them out of Egypt,
> because they did not remain faithful to my covenant,
>   and I turned away from them,
> declares the Lord.
>
> ¹⁰This is the covenant I will establish with the people of Israel
>   after that time, declares the Lord.
> I will put my laws in their minds
>   and write them on their hearts.
> I will be their God,
>   and they will be my people.
>
> ¹¹No longer will they teach their neighbor,
>   or say to one another, 'Know the Lord,'
> because they will all know me,
>   from the least of them to the greatest.
>
> ¹²For I will forgive their wickedness
>   and will remember their sins no more." *[Jeremiah 31:31-34]*

¹³In that he says, "A new covenant", he has made the first old. But that which is becoming old and grows aged is near to vanishing away.

God did not plan to restore some old covenant. God planned a new covenant. Laws would be written on the hearts of His people—the Church. These are bound to His Son in a marriage covenant.

Revelation 19:7-9 (ESV)

⁷Let us rejoice and exult and give him the glory, for the marriage of the Lamb has come, and his Bride has made herself ready; ⁸it was granted her to clothe herself with fine linen, bright and pure"-- for the fine linen is the righteous deeds of the saints. ⁹And the angel said to me, "Write this: Blessed are those who are invited to the marriage supper of the Lamb." And he said to me, "These are the true words of God."

Any good earthly marriage involves promises that are kept. Jesus is in the ultimate position to keep his promises which He has made to His bride, the church. His ability to fulfill his marriage vows is strong by reason of His eternal power and eternal love.

What is the Sword of the Spirit saying to we who have ears?

40
What More Can We Ask For?

Hebrews 10:11–18 (NIV)

[11]Day after day every priest stands and performs his religious duties; again and again he offers the same sacrifices, which can never take away sins. [12]But when this priest had offered for all time one sacrifice for sins, he sat down at the right hand of God, [13]and since that time he waits for his enemies to be made his footstool. [14]For by one sacrifice he has made perfect forever those who are being made holy.

[15]The Holy Spirit also testifies to us about this. First he says:

> [16]"This is the covenant I will make with them
> after that time, says the Lord.
> I will put my laws in their hearts,
> and I will write them on their minds." *[Jeremiah 31:33]*

[17]Then he adds,

> "Their sins and lawless acts
> I will remember no more." *[Jeremiah 31:34]*

[18]And where these have been forgiven, sacrifice for sin is no longer necessary.

If you've been perfected forever and you are being made holy (Hebrews 10:14), what work could "another Jesus" do that hasn't already been done? What more could you ask for?

Here's what we cannot ask for; we cannot ask for the world.

1 John 2:15 (NIV)

> Do not love the world or anything in the world. If anyone loves the world, love for the Father is not in them.

What is the Sword of the Spirit saying to we who have ears?

41
Equality

John 5:17–18 (NIV)

¹⁷In his defense Jesus said to them, "My Father is always at his work to this very day, and I too am working." ¹⁸For this reason they tried all the more to kill him; not only was he breaking the Sabbath, but he was even calling God his own Father, making himself equal with God.

They (the Jewish leadership) were half-right, right that Jesus claimed equality with God the Father. They were wrong not to believe Him.

What is the Sword of the Spirit saying to we who have ears?

42
Dead Raisers

John 5:21 (NIV)

For just as the Father raises the dead and gives them life, even so the Son gives life to whom he is pleased to give it.

The Father raises the dead. One dramatic example is what happened in the valley of the dry bones (Ezekiel 37).

Because Jesus is equal with the Father (John 5:17–18), it is not surprising that He also raises the dead. One dramatic example was in Nain, where Jesus raised the widow's son (Luke 7:11–17).

What is the Sword of the Spirit saying to we who have ears?

43
Two Roadblocks to Life

John 5:24–25 (NIV)

²⁴"Very truly I tell you, whoever **hears my word** and **believes him who sent me** has eternal life and will not be judged but has crossed over from death to life. ²⁵Very truly I tell you, a time is coming and has now come when the dead will hear the voice of the Son of God and those who hear will live.

Jesus offers eternal life. Two things could stand in our way:

1. Ignoring Jesus' words, and
2. Unbelief in the Father who sent Jesus.

A common way people ignore Jesus' words is by following after the false "christs." Jesus warned us of these (Matthew 24:24). This Jesus is the only Christ (1 Timothy 2:5; Jude 1:4).

What is the Sword of the Spirit saying to we who have ears?

44
Authority and Power: All of It

Matthew 28:18 (NIV)

Then Jesus came to them and said, "All authority* in heaven and on earth has been given to me.

Known as the 'Great Commission,' Jesus prefaced this message to His disciples with the above reminder about His authority.

Does Jesus have authority over life? Over death? Over heaven? Over hell? Over Angels? Over Satan?

"Yes" is the answer to all these questions.

What is the Sword of the Spirit saying to we who have ears?

---

* ἐξουσία is the Greek word translated as both 'Authority' and 'Power' (69x and 29x, respectively, in the King James Version New Testament).

45
A Powerful Commission for Saul of Tarsus

Acts 26:15–18 (NIV)

¹⁵"Then I asked, 'Who are you, Lord?'

" 'I am Jesus, whom you are persecuting,' the Lord replied. ¹⁶'Now get up and stand on your feet. I have appeared to you to appoint you as a servant and as a witness of what you have seen and will see of me. ¹⁷I will rescue you from your own people and from the Gentiles. I am sending you to them ¹⁸to open their eyes and turn them from darkness to light, and from the power* of Satan to God, so that they may receive forgiveness of sins and a place among those who are sanctified by faith in me.'"

Even Saul (a.k.a. Paul) received the "Great Commission," just as the other apostles did earlier. Jesus gives His commission with "all authority" (Matthew 28:18–20)—this authority is more than sufficient to overpower Satan.

What is the Sword of the Spirit saying to we who have ears?

---

* ἐξουσία is the Greek word translated to English alternatives 'Authority' and 'Power' (69x and 29x, respectively, in the King James Version New Testament); it is used in both Matthew 28:18 and Acts 26:18.

46
Big Miracle or Small?

John 6:5–6, 8–11 (NIV)

⁵When Jesus looked up and saw a great crowd coming toward him, he said to Philip, "Where shall we buy bread for these people to eat?" ⁶He asked this only to test him, for he already had in mind what he was going to do. ⁷Philip answered him, "It would take more than half a year's wages to buy enough bread for each one to have a bite!"

⁸Another of his disciples, Andrew, Simon Peter's brother, spoke up, ⁹"Here is a boy with five small barley loaves and two small fish, but how far will they go among so many?"

¹⁰Jesus said, "Have the people sit down." There was plenty of grass in that place, and they sat down (about five thousand men were there). ¹¹Jesus then took the loaves, gave thanks, and distributed to those who were seated as much as they wanted. He did the same with the fish.

All of Jesus' signs are "big" from our human vantage point because all of them are supernatural. But from Jesus' perspective, feeding 5,000 men could be seen as insignificant. It would be insignificant when compared with the time He sustained a million+ Israelites in the wilderness for 40 years (1 Corinthians 10:4).

What is the Sword of the Spirit saying to we who have ears?

47
Christians Have Reason for Great Expectations

1 Peter 1:3-9 (NIV)

³Praise be to the God and Father of our Lord Jesus Christ! In his great mercy **he has given us new birth into a living hope** through the resurrection of Jesus Christ from the dead, ⁴and into **an inheritance that can never perish, spoil or fade. This inheritance is kept in heaven for you,** ⁵**who** through faith **are shielded by God's power** until the coming of the salvation that is ready to be revealed in the last time. ⁶In all this you greatly rejoice, though now for a little while you may have had to suffer grief in all kinds of trials. ⁷These have come so that the proven genuineness of your faith—**of greater worth than gold, which perishes even though refined by fire**—may result in praise, glory and honor when Jesus Christ is revealed. ⁸Though you have not seen him, you love him; and even though you do not see him now, you believe in him and are filled with an inexpressible and glorious joy, ⁹for you are receiving the end result of your faith, the salvation of your souls.

Many seek gold. Gold is impressive; we refine it by fire and it survives. But gold will perish, "even though refined by fire," when the heavens and earth pass away (Matthew 24:35).

Christians hope in God, their Father, who promises them an inheritance. "Inheritance," happens within families. Christians enter God's family through the "new birth", through "Baptism" into the Father's only son (Galatians 3:26–27). This inheritance is kept safe in God's heaven; that's the only heaven which will not pass away.

It sure beats gold.

What is the Sword of the Spirit saying to we who have ears?

❦ 48 ❦
God's Power, Strongest!
God's Wisdom, Wisest!

1 Corinthians 1:18–25 (NIV)

¹⁸For **the message of the cross is foolishness to those who are perishing, but to us who are being saved it is the power of God.** ¹⁹For it is written:

"I will destroy the wisdom of the wise;
  the intelligence of the intelligent I will frustrate." [Isaiah 29:14]

²⁰Where is the wise person? Where is the teacher of the law? Where is the philosopher of this age? Has not God made foolish the wisdom of the world? ²¹For since in the wisdom of God the world through its wisdom did not know him, **God was pleased through the foolishness of what was preached to save those who believe.** ²²Jews demand signs and Greeks look for wisdom, ²³but **we preach Christ crucified:** a stumbling block to Jews and foolishness to Gentiles, ²⁴but to those whom God has called, both Jews and Greeks, **Christ the power of God and the wisdom of God.** ²⁵**For the foolishness of God is wiser** than human wisdom, and **the weakness of God is stronger** than human strength.

God is very pleased with what Paul and the other Christians preach. "Christ crucified" pleases the Father. Preaching the crucified Christ glorifies God because it makes known God's power and God's wisdom. It can't get any more powerful or wiser than God's plan of the cross.

What is the Sword of the Spirit saying to we who have ears?

49
The Cornerstone: The God-Laid Stone for The Stone-Saved Church

1 Peter 2:4-10 (NIV)

⁴As you come to him, the living Stone—rejected by humans but chosen by God and precious to him— ⁵you also, like living stones, are being built into a spiritual house to be a holy priesthood, offering spiritual sacrifices acceptable to God through Jesus Christ. ⁶For in Scripture it says:

> "See, I lay a stone in Zion,
>   a chosen and precious cornerstone,
> and the one who trusts in him
>   will never be put to shame." *[Isaiah 28:16]*

⁷Now to you who believe, this stone is precious. But to those who do not believe,

> "The stone the builders rejected
>   has become the cornerstone," *[Psalm 118:22]*

⁸and,

> "A stone that causes people to stumble
>   and a rock that makes them fall." *[Isaiah 8:14]*

They stumble because they disobey the message—which is also what they were destined for.

⁹But you are a chosen people, a royal priesthood, a holy nation, God's special possession, that you may declare the praises of him who called you out of darkness into his wonderful light. ¹⁰Once you were not a people, but now you are the people of God; once you had not received mercy, but now you have received mercy.

Within God's awesome plan, stumblers were destined to stumble. But those willing to come to this living Stone (vs. 4) are in the church of Christ; they are being built into living stones. We proclaim the excellencies of this Stone who called us out of darkness.

How wonderful is that stone?

Though rejected by men, Jesus Christ is chosen and precious in God's eyes—It can't get more wonderful!

What is the Sword of the Spirit saying to we who have ears?

50
First Importance

1 Corinthians 15:1–5 (NIV)

¹Now, brothers and sisters, I want to remind you of the **gospel** I **preached** to you, which you **received** and on which you have taken your **stand**. ²By this gospel you are **saved**, if you hold firmly to the word I preached to you. **Otherwise**, you have **believed in vain.**

³For what I received I passed on to you as of first importance: that Christ **died** for our sins **according to the Scriptures**, ⁴that he was **buried**, that he was **raised** on the third day **according to the Scriptures**, ⁵and **that he appeared** to Cephas, and then to the Twelve.

The Holy Spirit is speaking of life and death matters, matters of salvation.

This gospel (Good News) is of first importance. Paul outlines that gospel starting in verse 3.

1. Christ died for our sins (according to the Scriptures),
2. He was buried,
3. He was raised on the 3rd day (according to the Scriptures),
4. He appeared (there were witnesses to his bodily resurrection)

What is the Sword of the Spirit saying to we who have ears?

51
Good Intentions

Ephesians 3:9b–11 (NIV)

⁹ᵇ·God, who created all things. ¹⁰**His intent was that now, through the church**, the manifold wisdom of God should be made known to the rulers and authorities in the heavenly realms, ¹¹**according to his eternal purpose that he accomplished in Christ Jesus our Lord.**

At times I've been asked, "What was God's original intention or purpose?" The Holy Spirit has revealed it. What God intended is made known through the church. What God purposed has never changed; it is eternal. God accomplished His purpose through a specific Jesus—the Lord of His church whom He purchased with through Jesus' own blood.

What is the Sword of the Spirit saying to we who have ears?

52
Eternal Light, Eternal Life

John 8:12 (NIV)

When Jesus spoke again to the people, he said, "**I am** the **light of the world**. Whoever follows **me** will never walk in darkness, but will have the **light of life**."

Jesus identifies whom we must follow; "It's me." We are to follow the Jesus who spoke these words. Only the Jesus who spoke these words ~2000 years ago *is the light* and *gives life*. Jesus warned against others claiming the same.

Luke 21:8 (NIV)

He replied: "Watch out that you are not deceived. For many will come in my name, claiming, 'I am he,' and, 'The time is near.' Do not follow them."

What is the Sword of the Spirit saying to we who have ears?

53
Revealing Jesus' Identity

John 8:28 (NIV)

So Jesus said, "When you have lifted up the Son of Man, then you will know that I am he and that I do nothing on my own but speak just what the Father has taught me.

Jesus spoke to Jews who rejected His authority. It is through being lifted up on the cross* that Jesus reveals himself. His cross and resurrection prove his identity. Jesus had been stating his identity five verses earlier.

John 8:23 (NIV)

But he continued, "You are from below; I am from above. You are of this world; I am not of this world.

Jesus is unique. All humanity is from below, conceived on earth. Even Adam was from the dust of the ground and Eve from Adam's rib on earth. But Jesus is from out of this world.

What is the Sword of the Spirit saying to we who have ears?

---

* "Lifted up" indicates the cross. John 12:32–33, "'And I, when I am lifted up from the earth, will draw all people to myself.' He said this to show by what kind of death He was going to die."

54
Rebuilt by the Manufacturer

John 9:1, 5–7 (NIV)

As he went along, he saw a man blind from birth. ... ⁵While I am in the world, I am the light of the world." ⁶After saying this, **he spit on the ground, made some mud with the saliva, and put it on the man's eyes.** ⁷"Go," he told him, "wash in the Pool of Siloam" (this word means "Sent"). So the man went and washed, and came home seeing.

When I get something in my eye, it stings; it can cause damage or infection. The last thing I want in my eye is spit and mud. But the technique Jesus used shouldn't suprise us because Jesus made the very first eyes in a similar way.

Genesis 2:7 (NIV)

Then the Lord God formed a man from the dust of the ground and breathed into his nostrils the breath of life, and the man became a living being.

Jesus made eyes from scratch. I assume that's because the blind man's eyes were too damaged. Jesus just made them the way He did when He created man the first time, from the dust of the ground.

What is the Sword of the Spirit saying to we who have ears?

55
Atonement

1 John 4:7–10 (NIV)

⁷Dear friends, let us love one another, for love comes from God. Everyone who loves has been born of God and knows God. ⁸Whoever does not love does not know God, because God is love. ⁹This is how God showed his love among us: He sent his one and only Son into the world that we might live through him. ¹⁰This is love: not that we loved God, but that he loved us and sent his Son as an atoning sacrifice for our sins.

This is such a humbling passage. God's love is showered on Christians, because they receive the blessing of the atoning sacrifice Jesus made for sins. It's the Father's love in sending; it's the Son's love in taking on the mission.

—Roger Clevenger[*]

What is the Sword of the Spirit saying to we who have ears?

---

[*] This devotional though was contributed by my friend Roger Clevenger, along with a second one that can be found in the addendum of this book.

❦ 56 ❦
The One Man Worthy of Worship

John 9:32–38 (NIV)

[*Former blind man*]: Nobody has ever heard of opening the eyes of a man born blind. If this man were not from God, he could do nothing."

[*Pharisees*]: To this they replied, "You were steeped in sin at birth; how dare you lecture us!" And they threw him out.

Jesus heard that they had thrown him out, and when he found him, he said, "Do you believe in **the Son of Man**?"

[*Former blind man*]: "Who is he, sir?" the man asked. "Tell me so that I may believe in him."

Jesus said, "You have now seen him; in fact, **he is the one speaking** with you."

[*Former blind man*]: Then the man said, **"Lord, I believe,"** and *he worshiped him.*

Because Jesus is the singular "Son of Man," that unique "Son of Man," He is worthy of receiving worship. His is a special case, which is made clear in these passages: (a) John was forbidden to worship an angel (Revelation 19:9–10); (b) Paul and Barnabas refused to be treated as deities (Acts 14:13–18); (c) Peter refused to be worshiped by Cornelius (Acts 10:26); (d) Jesus reminded Satan that only God can be worshiped (Matthew 4:10).

But this "Son of Man," this Jesus, can accept worship. Therefore He is divine. That is consistent with the truth that "only God can be worshiped." He is worshiped because this "Son of Man" is one with the Father*, one with God.

What is the Sword of the Spirit saying to we who have ears?

---

* John 10:30 (ESV) — "I and the Father are one."

57
The Father Reacts to the Cross

John 10:17–18 (NIV)

¹⁷**The reason my Father loves me is that I lay down my life**—only to take it up again. ¹⁸No one takes it from me, but I lay it down of my own accord. I have authority to lay it down and authority to take it up again. **This command I received from my Father."**

Suppose Jesus failed to lay down his life, what then? He would be disobeying the command He received from the Father; that would be rebellion.

What is the Father's reaction to Jesus' decision to lay down His life? The Father loves Him because of it.

Love is the Father's reaction even before Jesus followed through on the plan of the cross.

What is the Sword of the Spirit saying to we who have ears?

58
Jesus Self-Resurrects

John 10:17–18 (NIV)

¹⁷The reason my Father loves me is that **I lay down my life—only to take it up again.** ¹⁸No one takes it from me, but I lay it down of my own accord. **I have authority to lay it down and authority to take it up again.** This command I received from my Father."

Jesus predicts that he will perform his own resurrection. He also predicted this when he cleared the temple of money changers (John 2:18-22). Only God can self-resurrect.

Resurrection is rare. It should be especially difficult doing it yourself – as death appears to be a handicap all-round. So, it would seem more natural to hear that "The Father" raises Jesus.

I have found eighteen other passages describing his resurrection as being performed by "God" or "the Father".

But these two passages need not be seen as a discrepancy. We must recall that Jesus said: "I and the Father are one," (John 10:30).

What is the Sword of the Spirit saying to we who have ears?

59
Jesus Has My Problems Nailed

Hebrews 10:8–10 (NIV)

⁸First he said, "Sacrifices and offerings, burnt offerings and sin offerings you did not desire, nor were you pleased with them"—though they were offered in accordance with the law. ⁹Then he said, "**Here I am, I have come to do your will.**" He sets aside the first to establish the second. ¹⁰And **by that will, we have been made holy through the sacrifice of the body of Jesus Christ once for all.**

Jesus was *willing* to be nailed to the cross. The Father was *willing* that Jesus be nailed to the cross. Jesus' church is made holy by these nails, the cross, those wounds, and that blood.

What is the Sword of the Spirit saying to we who have ears?

60
Powerful Hand

John 10:27–30 (NIV)

²⁷My sheep listen to my voice; I know them, and they follow me. ²⁸I give them eternal life, and they shall never perish; **no one will snatch them out of my hand.** ²⁹My Father, who has given them to me, is greater than all; **no one can snatch them out of my Father's hand.** ³⁰**I and the Father are one."**

The Father's hand is powerful. Jesus' hand is equally powerful. They are one.

What is the Sword of the Spirit saying to we who have ears?

61
A Just Stoning?

John 10:30–33 (NIV)

³⁰"I and the Father are one."

³¹Again his Jewish opponents picked up stones to stone him, ³²but Jesus said to them, "I have shown you many good works from the Father. For which of these do you stone me?"

³³"We are not stoning you for any good work," they replied, "but for blasphemy, because you, a mere man, claim to be God."

Some of Jesus' own countrymen ("Jewish opponents") sought righteous justice by attempting to stone Him to death. If Jesus were not actually God, they would have been justified in executing Him (Leviticus 24:16).

They clearly understood Jesus' claims. But their reaction was not justified. In part, it was unjustified because of the miraculous "good works" that Jesus performed. These works declared them to be "unjust" in their desire to stone Him.

What is the Sword of the Spirit saying to we who have ears?

62
Resurrection Day and Life

John 11:24–27 (NIV)

²⁴Martha answered, "I know he will rise again in **the resurrection at the last day.**"

²⁵Jesus said to her, "**I am the resurrection and the life.** The one who believes in me will live, even though they die; ²⁶and whoever lives by believing in me will never die. Do you believe this?"

²⁷"Yes, Lord," she replied, "I believe that you are the Messiah, the Son of God, who is to come into the world."

Martha surely knew of resurrections in the scriptures, such as the ones that God performed through Elijah and Elisha. But Martha is clearly specifying a future resurrection, "at the last day." This sounds more like Daniel 12:13 – *As for you, go your way till the end. You will rest, and then at the end of the days you will rise to receive your allotted inheritance.* (NIV)

Yet the resurrection is more than a final judgment day, it is also a person. It is this Jesus who is also "The Life."

What is the Sword of the Spirit saying to we who have ears?

63
The High Priest Prophesies

John 11:47–53 (NIV)

⁴⁷Then the chief priests and the Pharisees called a meeting of the Sanhedrin.

"What are we accomplishing?" they asked. "Here is this man performing many signs. ⁴⁸If we let him go on like this, everyone will believe in him, and then the Romans will come and take away both our temple and our nation."

⁴⁹Then one of them, named Caiaphas, who was high priest that year, spoke up, "You know nothing at all! ⁵⁰**You do not realize that it is better for you that one man die for the people than that the whole nation perish.**"

⁵¹He did not say this on his own, but **as high priest that year he prophesied that Jesus would die for the Jewish nation, ⁵²and not only for that nation but also for the scattered children of God, to bring them together and make them one.** ⁵³So from that day on they plotted to take his life.

Caiaphas predicts the death of Jesus, as well as the purpose of His death: so that not all the nation of Israel should perish.

Nevertheless, the blessings of Jesus' death extend beyond Israel's borders: "not only for that nation but also for the scattered children of God." God created all men in His image. It is all nations, not just the nation of the Jews, who can receive the blessings of Jesus' death.

What is the Sword of the Spirit saying to we who have ears?

64
Without His Glory, the Real Jesus Can't Be Seen

John 12:20–26 (NIV)

[20]Now there were some Greeks among those who went up to worship at the festival. [21]They came to Philip, who was from Bethsaida in Galilee, with a request. "Sir," they said, "we would like to see Jesus." [22]Philip went to tell Andrew; Andrew and Philip in turn told Jesus.

[23]Jesus replied, "The hour has come for the Son of Man to be glorified. [24]Very truly I tell you, unless a kernel of wheat falls to the ground and dies, it remains only a single seed. But if it dies, it produces many seeds. [25]Anyone who loves their life will lose it, while anyone who hates their life in this world will keep it for eternal life. [26]Whoever serves me must follow me; and where I am, my servant also will be. My Father will honor the one who serves me.

These Greeks want to see Jesus. Jesus reveals His glorious hour as being "The Son of Man." That's how they'll begin to see Jesus: dying, losing life in this world, and providing eternal life. The cross is Jesus' glory, the crucial element making Him visible. Then Jesus invites us all to follow Him through death into life eternal.

What is the Sword of the Spirit saying to we who have ears?

65
The Father Confirms the Son's Purpose

John 12:27–33 (NIV)

²⁷"Now my soul is troubled, and what shall I say? 'Father, save me from this hour'? **No, it was for this very reason I came to this hour.** ²⁸Father, glorify your name!"

Then a voice came from heaven, "I have glorified it, and will glorify it again." ²⁹The crowd that was there and heard it said it had thundered; others said an angel had spoken to him.

³⁰Jesus said, "This voice was for your benefit, not mine. ³¹Now is the time for judgment on this world; now the prince of this world will be driven out. ³²**And I, when I am lifted up from the earth, will draw all people to myself.**" ³³**He said this to show the kind of death he was going to die.**

Jesus did not ask the Father to save Him from "This Hour"; He stays true to His mission on earth. The Father responds aloud, confirming that He shares this glorious purpose with His Son. Jesus plainly restates the mission: to be lifted up from the earth, upon the cross, so as to draw all people to Himself.

What is the Sword of the Spirit saying to we who have ears?

66
Predicting Blessings (But Not for All)

John 13:17–19 (NIV)

¹⁷Now that you know these things, you will be blessed if you do them.

¹⁸"I am not referring to all of you; I know those I have chosen. But this is to fulfill this passage of Scripture: 'He who shared my bread has turned against me.'

¹⁹"I am telling you now before it happens, so that when it does happen you will believe that I am who I am.

Jesus predicts a couple things. The first is a conditional prediction: "you will be blessed" on the condition that "you do" these things. One of those who will not be blessed is the traitor, Judas ("I am not referring to all of you").

Jesus predicts his betrayal and emphasizes that this had also been predicted by Scripture (Psalm 41:9).

What is the Sword of the Spirit saying to we who have ears?

❦ 67 ❦
The Invisible Made Visible

John 14:7–10 (NIV)

⁷If you really know me, you will know my Father as well. From now on, you do know him and have seen him."

⁸Philip said, "Lord, show us the Father and that will be enough for us."

⁹Jesus answered: "Don't you know me, Philip, even after I have been among you such a long time? Anyone who has seen me has seen the Father. How can you say, 'Show us the Father'? ¹⁰Don't you believe that I am in the Father, and that the Father is in me? The words I say to you I do not speak on my own authority. Rather, it is the Father, living in me, who is doing his work.

If you are searching for God, it is through Jesus that you'll be able to see Him. Without Jesus, God is invisible (Colossians 1:15; 1 Timothy 1:17).

What is the Sword of the Spirit saying to we who have ears?

❦ 68 ❦
He Came from Beyond the Blue

John 16:28–30 (NIV)

²⁸I came from the Father and entered the world; now I am leaving the world and going back to the Father."

²⁹Then Jesus' disciples said, "Now you are speaking clearly and without figures of speech. ³⁰Now we can see that you know all things and that you do not even need to have anyone ask you questions. This makes us believe that you came from God."

Jesus spoke both plainly and with symbolic language. Here, Jesus speaks plainly. Only Jesus has come from God and entered the world. The rest of us were born here.

What is the Sword of the Spirit saying to we who have ears?

69
Men Granted Peacemaking Authority

John 20:19–23 (NIV)

¹⁹On the evening of that first day of the week, when the disciples were together, with the doors locked for fear of the Jewish leaders, Jesus came and stood among them and said, "Peace be with you!" ²⁰After he said this, he showed them his hands and side. **The disciples were overjoyed when they saw the Lord.**

²¹Again Jesus said, "Peace be with you! **As the Father has sent me, I am sending you.**" ²²And with that he breathed on them and said, "Receive the Holy Spirit. ²³If you forgive anyone's sins, their sins are forgiven; if you do not forgive them, they are not forgiven."

These men were overjoyed after they saw Jesus' nail scarred hands and side. They were joyful because they knew He was their Jesus, the one who had endured the cross and overcome the grave.

But with this knowledge comes great responsibility. They have a message that means the difference between forgiveness and damnation. Jesus is sending them with the saving gospel—saving good news.

What is the Sword of the Spirit saying to we who have ears?

70
King Jesus, the Goal of Truth-Seekers

John 18:35–37 (NIV)

³⁵"Am I a Jew?" Pilate replied. "Your own people and chief priests handed you over to me. What is it you have done?"

³⁶Jesus said, "**My kingdom is not of this world.** If it were, my servants would fight to prevent my arrest by the Jewish leaders. But now **my kingdom is from another place.**"

³⁷"**You are a king, then!**" said Pilate.

Jesus answered, "You say that I am a king. In fact, **the reason I was born and came into the world is to testify to the truth. Everyone on the side of truth listens to me.**"

So many tend to think of themselves as being on the side of truth. If that really is the case, these people should be listening to King Jesus.

He testifies to The Truth and He is the Truth.

John 14:6 (NIV)

Jesus said to him, "I am the way, and the truth, and the life; no one comes to the Father but through Me.

What is the Sword of the Spirit saying to we who have ears?

71
Strategy for World-Blessing

John 17:15–24 (NIV)

¹⁵My prayer is not that you take them out of the world but that you protect them from the evil one. **¹⁶They are not of the world, even as I am not of it. ¹⁷Sanctify them by the truth; your word is truth. ¹⁸As you sent me into the world, I have sent them into the world.** ¹⁹For them I sanctify myself, that they too may be truly sanctified.

²⁰"My prayer is not for them alone. I pray also for those who will believe in me through their message, ²¹that all of them may be one, Father, just as you are in me and I am in you. May they also be in us so that the world may believe that you have sent me. ²²I have given them the glory that you gave me, that they may be one as we are one— ²³I in them and you in me—so that they may be brought to complete unity. Then the world will know that you sent me and have loved them even as you have loved me.

²⁴"Father, **I want those** you have given me to be with me where I am, and **to see my glory, the glory you have given me because you loved me before the creation of the world.**

King Jesus is sending his disciples into the world to bless it. Though these eleven would die, the mission continues through those who obey that message which the eleven passed along.

This is the strategy Jesus repeated when he gave them the "Great Commission," saying,

> "Therefore, go and make disciples of all nations, baptizing them in the name of the Father and of the Son and of the Holy Spirit, and teaching them to obey everything I have commanded you." *[Matthew 28:19–20]*

"Sanctify them by the truth; your word is truth;" that worked for the eleven, and it works for us. It makes us victorious in our mission to the world.

John 17:24 (NIV)

> "Father, I want those you have given me to be with me where I am, and to see my glory, the glory you have given me because you loved me *before the creation of the world.*"

Those from the world, who have been placed in Christ Jesus, will see His glory. That's prehistoric glory!

What is the Sword of the Spirit saying to we who have ears?

72
Pilate, the Right Man for the Time

John 19:6–13 (NIV)

⁶As soon as the chief priests and their officials saw him, they shouted, "Crucify! Crucify!"

But Pilate answered, "You take him and crucify him. As for me, I find no basis for a charge against him."

⁷The Jewish leaders insisted, "We have a law, and according to that law he must die, because he claimed to be the Son of God."

⁸When Pilate heard this, he was even more afraid, ⁹and he went back inside the palace. "Where do you come from?" he asked Jesus, but Jesus gave him no answer. ¹⁰"Do you refuse to speak to me?" Pilate said. "Don't you realize I have power either to free you or to crucify you?"

¹¹Jesus answered, "You would have no power over me if it were not given to you from above. Therefore the one who handed me over to you is guilty of a greater sin."

¹²From then on, Pilate tried to set Jesus free, but the Jewish leaders kept shouting, "If you let this man go, you are no friend of Caesar. Anyone who claims to be a king opposes Caesar."

¹³When Pilate heard this, he brought Jesus out and sat down on the judge's seat at a place known as the Stone Pavement (which in Aramaic is Gabbatha).

Pilate, as the Roman governor, should have been able to exercise his power over the Jews. Yet the corrupt Jewish leadership put Pilate in a political no-win trap; he couldn't free Jesus without becoming a traitor to Caesar.

This was God's doing. The Father only gave Pilate the power to sentence Jesus to the cross. Pilate fought to free Jesus, but he was fighting against God's will. Pilate's failure to free Jesus was just what God had in mind.

What is the Sword of the Spirit saying to we who have ears?

73
My Lord and My God!

John 20:24–29 (NIV)

[24]Now Thomas (also known as Didymus), one of the Twelve, was not with the disciples when Jesus came. [25]So the other disciples told him, "We have seen the Lord!"

But he said to them, "Unless I see the nail marks in his hands and put my finger where the nails were, and put my hand into his side, I will not believe."

[26]A week later his disciples were in the house again, and Thomas was with them. Though the doors were locked, Jesus came and stood among them and said, "Peace be with you!" [27]Then he said to Thomas, "**Put your finger here; see my hands. Reach out your hand and put it into my side. Stop doubting and believe.**"

[28]Thomas said to him, "**My Lord and my God!**"

[29]Then Jesus told him, "Because you have seen me, you have believed; blessed are those who have not seen and yet have believed."

Thomas is not speaking to the Father; Thomas is addressing Jesus when he declares Him to be both his Lord and his God. Thomas has good reasons.

Thomas was an eye-witness, an ear-witness, and a touch-witness to the divinity of Jesus.

Jesus affirms Thomas' belief in Jesus' deity and then proceeds to bless all others who believe likewise. This is yet another instance of Jesus claiming to be God.

May all desire the blessing that goes with believing Jesus is God.

What is the Sword of the Spirit saying to we who have ears?

74
Jesus, the Good Shepherd

Psalm 23:1–2 (KJV)

¹The Lord is my shepherd; I shall not want. ²He maketh me to lie down in green pastures: he leadeth me beside the still waters.

Ezekiel 34:15–16 (NIV)

¹⁵I myself will tend my sheep and have them lie down, declares the Sovereign Lord. ¹⁶I will search for the lost and bring back the strays. I will bind up the injured and strengthen the weak, but the sleek and the strong I will destroy. I will shepherd the flock with justice.

Ezekiel 34:31 (NIV)

³¹You are my sheep, the sheep of my pasture, and I am your God, declares the Sovereign Lord.'"

John 10:11 (NIV)

¹¹"I am the good shepherd. The good shepherd lays down his life for the sheep.

King Jesus is king David's shepherd. King Jesus is our shepherd. He binds up the injured and strengthens the weak. He laid down His life for us.

Jesus is also the shepherd of justice. The proud, the sleek and the strong, He will destroy. If we become proud, He will destroy us as well.

What is the Sword of the Spirit saying to we who have ears?

75
Yahweh's Path Has Been Prepared

Mark 1:1–4 (NIV)

The beginning of the good news about Jesus the Messiah, the Son of God, ²as it is written in Isaiah the prophet:

> "I will send my messenger ahead of you,
>   who will prepare your way"—
> ³"a voice of one calling in the wilderness,
> 'Prepare the way for the Lord,
>   make straight paths for him.'" *[Isaiah 40:3]*

⁴And so John the Baptist appeared in the wilderness, preaching a baptism of repentance for the forgiveness of sins.

John the Baptist prepared someone's way. To uncover his identity, we are directed to the prophet Isaiah. Looking closely, at the same passage in the Old Testament, we notice that the word "Lord" (New Testament) has been reproduced with small caps, typeset as LORD, rather than using any lower case letter.

Isaiah 40:3 (NIV)

A voice of one calling: "In the wilderness prepare the way for the Lord; make straight in the desert a highway for our God.

Translators use this small-cap convention to indicate that this Lord (in contrast to "Lord") is the Hebrew word YHWH. When Moses was at the burning bush, he asked God for His name, YHWH is the personal name which He revealed to Moses

John the Baptist was preparing the way for YHWH, for God himself. It is "a highway for our God." In preparing the way for Jesus, John succeeded in his mission. Indeed, Jesus is YHWH. His very name, Jesus, ("Yeshua), is understood by the Jews to mean "YHWH saves." After Jesus' work is done, Earth, Heaven, and Hell will all know that "YHWH saves!"

What is the Sword of the Spirit saying to we who have ears?

76
Could the Son Have Made the Universe?

Hebrews 1:1–3 (NIV)

¹In the past God spoke to our ancestors through the prophets at many times and in various ways, ²but in these last days he has spoken to us by his Son, whom he appointed heir of all things, and through whom also he made the universe. ³The Son is the radiance of God's glory and the exact representation of his being, sustaining all things by his powerful word. After he had provided purification for sins, he sat down at the right hand of the Majesty in heaven.

Hebrews 1:8 (NIV)

⁸But about the Son he says,

> "Your throne, O God, will last for ever and ever; a scepter of justice will be the scepter of your kingdom. *[Psalm 45:6]*

Until we listen to what the Holy Spirit reveals about Jesus, it seems strange to think of God's Son as having created the universe. But it is not so strange when we learn that the Son is God. One place where The Holy Spirit reveals that the Son is God is Hebrews 1:8.

What is the Sword of the Spirit saying to we who have ears?

77
Whose Sabbath?

Mark 2:23–28 (NIV)

²³One Sabbath Jesus was going through the grainfields, and as his disciples walked along, they began to pick some heads of grain. ²⁴The Pharisees said to him, "Look, why are they doing what is unlawful on the Sabbath?"

²⁵He answered, "Have you never read what David did when he and his companions were hungry and in need? ²⁶In the days of Abiathar the high priest, he entered the house of God and ate the consecrated bread, which is lawful only for priests to eat. And he also gave some to his companions."

²⁷Then he said to them, "The Sabbath was made for man, not man for the Sabbath. ²⁸So the Son of Man is Lord even of the Sabbath."

The Sabbath was a holy day. God made it holy, setting it apart from other days to bless mankind. Sabbaths provide a weekly rest (Exodus 31:15); they prevent one man from overworking his fellow man. God claimed ownership of Sabbaths (Leviticus 19:3, "my Sabbaths").

Jesus claims to be "Lord" and "Lord even of the Sabbath." Jesus is not saying he's taking ownership away from God – Jesus is claiming to be God.

What is the Sword of the Spirit saying to we who have ears?

❦ 78 ❦
Holy Man and the Holier One

Mark 1:4–8 (NIV)

⁴John appeared, baptizing in the wilderness and proclaiming a baptism of repentance for the forgiveness of sins. ⁵And all the country of Judea and all Jerusalem were going out to him and were being baptized by him in the river Jordan, confessing their sins. ⁶Now John was clothed with camel's hair and wore a leather belt around his waist and ate locusts and wild honey. ⁷And he preached, saying, "After me comes he who is mightier than I, the strap of whose sandals I am not worthy to stoop down and untie. ⁸I have baptized you with water, but he will baptize you with the Holy Spirit."

John was holy. He was out in the wilderness and city dwellers flocked to him, confessing their sins. His message really resonated; he must have delivered the message with a holy lifestyle that backed it up.

The message contained more than condemnation; it also contained fear and hope. This was a message of fear for the coming of one infinitely greater than John, but also of hope for forgiveness and hope that the coming one would provide the Holy Spirit.

It's hard to imagine someone so worthy that this holy John would not be "worthy" enough to untie his sandals. But if that greater one is God, then that would make sense. It would also make sense that God should be the one providing the Holy Spirit.

What is the Sword of the Spirit saying to we who have ears?

79
Testimony by the Demons

Mark 1:23–28 (NIV)

23 Just then a man in their synagogue who was possessed by an impure spirit cried out, 24 "What do you want with us, Jesus of Nazareth? Have you come to destroy us? I know who you are—the Holy One of God!"

25 "Be quiet!" said Jesus sternly. "Come out of him!" 26 The impure spirit shook the man violently and came out of him with a shriek.

27 The people were all so amazed that they asked each other, "What is this? A new teaching—and with authority! He even gives orders to impure spirits and they obey him." 28 News about him spread quickly over the whole region of Galilee.

Mark 1:34 (NIV)

34 and Jesus healed many who had various diseases. He also drove out many demons, but he would not let the demons speak because they knew who he was.

Impure spirits and demons recognize Jesus' sonship, his holiness, his power, and his mission to destroy them and their power. Jesus' power over demons should not be a surprise when you recall that Jesus is God.

Additionally, we should not be surprised that the devils recognize Jesus. Being God, Jesus would have been involved with the judgment of Adam and Eve and the Serpent, back in Genesis 3:1-13. We could reasonably expect Jesus to have been present when God (the Father, the Son, and Holy Spirit) spoke with Satan in Job 1:6-2:7.

What is the Sword of the Spirit saying to we who have ears?

80
The Healing Voice of God

Mark 1:40–44 (ESV)

⁴⁰A man with leprosy came to him and begged him on his knees, "If you are willing, you can make me clean."

⁴¹Filled with compassion, Jesus reached out his hand and touched the man. "I am willing," he said. "Be clean!" ⁴²Immediately the leprosy left him and he was cured.

⁴³Jesus sent him away at once with a strong warning: ⁴⁴"See that you don't tell this to anyone. But go, show yourself to the priest and offer the sacrifices that Moses commanded for your cleansing, as a testimony to them."

The Hebrew God is known for compassion (Exodus 22:26-27, Psalm 103:13). A Syrian army commander, Naaman, was another leper who turned to The powerful God of the Hebrews for healing (2 Kings 5:1-14). In healing this man of leprosy, Jesus meets Hebrew expectations for deity in both compassion and healing power.

It is proper to ask why God would send the leper to the priest. Jesus was reminding the man to follow God's laws concerning cleansing from leprosy (Leviticus 14:2-32); God healed him so God must be thanked. Jesus is not going to disregard his own orders, the very laws which he had given Moses.

What is the Sword of the Spirit saying to we who have ears?

81
Divine Forgiveness

Mark 2:1–12 (NIV)

¹A few days later, when Jesus again entered Capernaum, the people heard that he had come home. ²They gathered in such large numbers that there was no room left, not even outside the door, and he preached the word to them. ³Some men came, bringing to him a paralyzed man, carried by four of them. ⁴Since they could not get him to Jesus because of the crowd, they made an opening in the roof above Jesus by digging through it and then lowered the mat the man was lying on. ⁵When Jesus saw their faith, he said to the paralyzed man, "Son, your sins are forgiven."

⁶Now some teachers of the law were sitting there, thinking to themselves, ⁷"Why does this fellow talk like that? He's blaspheming! Who can forgive sins but God alone?"

⁸Immediately Jesus knew in his spirit that this was what they were thinking in their hearts, and he said to them, "Why are you thinking these things? ⁹Which is easier: to say to this paralyzed man, 'Your sins are forgiven,' or to say, 'Get up, take your mat and walk'? ¹⁰But I want you to know that the Son of Man has authority on earth to forgive sins." So he said to the man, ¹¹"I tell you, get up, take your mat and go home." ¹²He got up, took his mat and walked out in full view of them all. This amazed everyone and they praised God, saying, "We have never seen anything like this!"

Sins can be forgiven only by the one sinned against. These Pharisees correctly assess the situation; if this paralyzed man has sinned, ultimately God must do the forgiving. There are at least two misunderstandings behind the Pharisees' blasphemy charge: a) that this paralyzed stranger has never sinned against Jesus personally and b) they assume Jesus is not God and so usurps God's role in forgiving.

It is only God who defines right and wrong, so all sin is against him. Ultimately, we must all seek God's forgiveness.

Jesus proves his divine authority to forgive sins by performing a divine healing.

What is the Sword of the Spirit saying to we who have ears?

82
Bride and Bridegroom

Mark 2:18-20 (NIV)

¹⁸Now John's disciples and the Pharisees were fasting. Some people came and asked Jesus, "How is it that John's disciples and the disciples of the Pharisees are fasting, but yours are not?"

¹⁹Jesus answered, "How can the guests of the bridegroom fast while he is with them? They cannot, so long as they have him with them. ²⁰But the time will come when the bridegroom will be taken from them, and on that day they will fast.

We must first see the strangeness of Jesus' answer before it can be better understood. Since we have no record of his betrothal, why would Jesus compare himself to a bridegroom? With Jesus as "the bridegroom" and His disciples as "friends of the bridegroom", who is the bride?

Pharisees were in the audience. They got Jesus' point. They knew, better than most, who the bride is.

Isaiah 62:1, 4–5 (NIV)

¹For Zion's sake I will not keep silent,
  for Jerusalem's sake I will not remain quiet,
till her vindication shines out like the dawn,
  her salvation like a blazing torch....
....⁴No longer will they call you Deserted,
  or name your land Desolate.
But you will be called Hephzibah,
  and your land Beulah;
for the LORD will take delight in you,
  and your land will be married.
⁵As a young man marries a young woman,
  so will your Builder marry you;
as a bridegroom rejoices over his bride,
  so will your God rejoice over you.

The bride is the people of Israel, so says the Holy Spirit through the prophet Isaiah. The LORD (The Builder, The Creator, and God) is going to marry his people. It's Jesus' wedding. Jesus is God.

What is the Sword of the Spirit saying to we who have ears?

83
Deep Distress, Deeply Troubled

Mark 3:1–6 (NIV)

¹Another time Jesus went into the synagogue, and a man with a shriveled hand was there. ²Some of them were looking for a reason to accuse Jesus, so they watched him closely to see if he would heal him on the Sabbath. ³Jesus said to the man with the shriveled hand, "Stand up in front of everyone."

⁴Then Jesus asked them, "Which is lawful on the Sabbath: to do good or to do evil, to save life or to kill?" But they remained silent.

⁵He looked around at them in anger and, deeply distressed at their stubborn hearts, said to the man, "Stretch out your hand." He stretched it out, and his hand was completely restored. ⁶Then the Pharisees went out and began to plot with the Herodians how they might kill Jesus.

Jesus was angry and deeply distressed at the stubborn hearts of some of the Pharisees in the synagogue. The cause of His distress was similar to they way He was deeply troubled during the days of Noah.

Genesis 6:5–8 (NIV)

⁵The Lord saw how great the wickedness of the human race had become on the earth, and that every inclination of the thoughts of the human heart was only evil all the time. ⁶The Lord regretted that he had made human beings on the earth, and his heart was deeply troubled. ⁷So the Lord said, "I will wipe from the face of the earth the human race I have created—and with them the animals, the birds and the creatures that move along the ground—for I regret that I have made them." ⁸But Noah found favor in the eyes of the Lord.

The deeply troubled heart was because the Lord, in His righteousness, had to destroy the world with water, except for Noah and his family. Jesus is similarly distressed in Mark 3:5. He knows, come judgment day, He will send those who reject him into eternal fire (Mark 9:42–50 "It is better for you to enter life crippled than with two hands to go to hell, to the unquenchable fire … thrown into hell … where the worm does not die and the fire is not quenched.")

Jesus does not enjoy this task; his heart was deeply troubled.

What is the Sword of the Spirit saying to we who have ears?

84
Kingdom Secrets

Mark 4:1–12 (ESV)

¹Again he began to teach beside the sea. And a very large crowd gathered about him, so that he got into a boat and sat in it on the sea, and the whole crowd was beside the sea on the land. ²And he was teaching them many things in parables, and in his teaching he said to them: ³"Listen! Behold, a sower went out to sow. ⁴And as he sowed, some seed fell along the path, and the birds came and devoured it. ⁵Other seed fell on rocky ground, where it did not have much soil, and immediately it sprang up, since it had no depth of soil. ⁶And when the sun rose, it was scorched, and since it had no root, it withered away. ⁷Other seed fell among thorns, and the thorns grew up and choked it, and it yielded no grain. ⁸And other seeds fell into good soil and produced grain, growing up and increasing and yielding thirtyfold and sixtyfold and a hundredfold." ⁹And he said, "He who has ears to hear, let him hear."

¹⁰And when he was alone, those around him with the twelve asked him about the parables. ¹¹And he said to them, "To you has been given the secret of the kingdom of God, but for those outside everything is in parables, ¹²so that "'they may indeed see but not perceive, and may indeed hear but not understand, lest they should turn and be forgiven.'"

Secrets: we are sometimes annoyed when we are not included. We are sometimes happy when the secrets are shared with us.

This parable of the soils was told to a crowd, but they did not understand. It was only revealed to the insiders. "Those outside" thought they were just hearing a story, one which did not pierce their hearts. But the twelve apostles sought out Jesus, who shared the secret contained within the parable—the secret of the kingdom of God. They ended up becoming insiders.

Want to know about God's kingdom? Then you will have to listen to Jesus' spokesmen, the apostles. They have the inside scoop, having received it straight from the mouth of God.

What is the Sword of the Spirit saying to we who have ears?

85

The Sea Master

Mark 4:35–41 (ESV)

³⁵On that day, when evening had come, he said to them, "Let us go across to the other side." ³⁶And leaving the crowd, they took him with them in the boat, just as he was. And other boats were with him. ³⁷And a great windstorm arose, and the waves were breaking into the boat, so that the boat was already filling. ³⁸But he was in the stern, asleep on the cushion. And they woke him and said to him, "Teacher, do you not care that we are perishing?" ³⁹And he awoke and rebuked the wind and said to the sea, "Peace! Be still!" And the wind ceased, and there was a great calm. ⁴⁰He said to them, "Why are you so afraid? Have you still no faith?" ⁴¹And they were filled with great fear and said to one another, "Who then is this, that even the wind and the sea obey him?"

Who then is this? There is only one who commands the sea. He revealed himself to the Jews. His name is Yahweh (LORD).

Psalm 107:28–30 (ESV)

²⁸Then they cried to the LORD in their trouble,
   and he delivered them from their distress.
²⁹He made the storm be still,
   and the waves of the sea were hushed.
³⁰Then they were glad that the waters were quiet,
   and he brought them to their desired haven.

What is the Sword of the Spirit saying to we who have ears?

❦ 86 ❦
Faithful to Jesus' Commission

Mark 5:5–20 (ESV)

⁵Night and day among the tombs and on the mountains he was always crying out and cutting himself with stones. ⁶And when he saw Jesus from afar, he ran and fell down before him. ⁷And crying out with a loud voice, he said, "What have you to do with me, Jesus, Son of the Most High God? I adjure you by God, do not torment me." ⁸For he was saying to him, "Come out of the man, you unclean spirit!" ⁹And Jesus asked him, "What is your name?" He replied, "My name is Legion, for we are many." ¹⁰And he begged him earnestly not to send them out of the country. ¹¹Now a great herd of pigs was feeding there on the hillside, ¹²and they begged him, saying, "Send us to the pigs; let us enter them." ¹³So he gave them permission. And the unclean spirits came out and entered the pigs; and the herd, numbering about two thousand, rushed down the steep bank into the sea and drowned in the sea. ¹⁴The herdsmen fled and told it in the city and in the country. And people came to see what it was that had happened. ¹⁵And they came to Jesus and saw the demon-possessed man, the one who had had the legion, sitting there, clothed and in his right mind, and they were afraid. ¹⁶And those who had seen it described to them what had happened to the demon-possessed man and to the pigs. ¹⁷And they began to beg Jesus to depart from their region. ¹⁸As he was getting into the boat, the man who had been possessed with demons begged him that he might be with him. ¹⁹And he did not permit him but said to him, "Go home to your friends and tell them how much the Lord has done for you, and how he has had mercy on you." ²⁰And he went away and began to proclaim in the Decapolis how much Jesus had done for him, and everyone marveled.

Here's a man who was in incomprehensible depths of despair. He had a legion's-worth of demons (about 6,000), until Jesus freed him.

Jesus gave the restored man a commission. Jesus's words and the manner of the man's obedience are significant; consider the details.

Jesus told him to tell his friends "how much **the Lord**" had done for him. The man went and told them "how much **Jesus** had done for him." The man was faithful to the commission because **Jesus is the Lord.**

What is the Sword of the Spirit saying to we who have ears?

87
Powerfully Placed Faith

Mark 5:27–34 (ESV)

²⁷She had heard the reports about Jesus and came up behind him in the crowd and touched his garment. ²⁸For she said, "If I touch even his garments, I will be made well." ²⁹And immediately the flow of blood dried up, and she felt in her body that she was healed of her disease. ³⁰And Jesus, perceiving in himself that power had gone out from him, immediately turned about in the crowd and said, "Who touched my garments?" ³¹And his disciples said to him, "You see the crowd pressing around you, and yet you say, 'Who touched me?'" ³²And he looked around to see who had done it. ³³But the woman, knowing what had happened to her, came in fear and trembling and fell down before him and told him the whole truth. ³⁴And he said to her, "Daughter, your faith has made you well; go in peace, and be healed of your disease."

A lot of people were hearing reports about Jesus' power, but this woman actually believed and acted on them. Though her faith is noteworthy, we should not make too much of it.

Faith is insufficient if placed in the wrong places. She was made well because her faith was placed in the only begotten Son of God—The Way, The Truth and The Life.

What is the Sword of the Spirit saying to we who have ears?

❦ 88 ❦
The Voice to Wake the Dead

Mark 5:38–42 (ESV)

^{38}They came to the house of the ruler of the synagogue [*Jairus*], and Jesus saw a commotion, people weeping and wailing loudly. ^{39}And when he had entered, he said to them, "Why are you making a commotion and weeping? The child is not dead but sleeping." ^{40}And they laughed at him. But he put them all outside and took the child's father and mother and those who were with him and went in where the child was. ^{41}Taking her by the hand he said to her, "Talitha cumi," which means, "Little girl, I say to you, arise." ^{42}And immediately the girl got up and began walking (for she was twelve years of age), and they were immediately overcome with amazement.

1 Thessalonians 4:13–16 (ESV)

^{13}But we do not want you to be uninformed, brothers, about those who are asleep, that you may not grieve as others do who have no hope. ^{14}For since we believe that Jesus died and rose again, even so, through Jesus, God will bring with him those who have fallen asleep. ^{15}For this we declare to you by a word from the Lord, that we who are alive, who are left until the coming of the Lord, will not precede those who have fallen asleep. ^{16}For the Lord himself will descend from heaven with a cry of command, with the voice of an archangel, and with the sound of the trumpet of God. And the dead in Christ will rise first.

Both passages discuss those who are truly dead. Both passages refer to the dead as being asleep. Sleep symbolizes Jairus' daughter's real death, as well as that of those who die physically within Christ. Those in Christ awaken from "sleep" through a real resurrection to eternal life.

There are others who will not awaken so happily. They are without hope, there is reason to grieve. Jesus of Nazareth, the Lord himself, is our only hope of resurrection and life.

What is the Sword of the Spirit saying to we who have ears?

89
Three Questions About Jesus

Mark 6:1–2 (ESV)

He [*Jesus*] went away from there and came to his hometown, and his disciples followed him. And on the Sabbath he began to teach in the synagogue, and many who heard him were astonished, saying, "Where did this man get these things? What is the wisdom given to him? How are such mighty works done by his hands?

1 joh

Three questions were asked. God provides answers.

1. "Where did this man get these things?"

Matthew 11:27 (ESV)

All things have been handed over to me by my Father, and no one knows the Son except the Father, and no one knows the Father except the Son and anyone to whom the Son chooses to reveal him.

He was handed all things by God the Father.

2. "What is the wisdom given to him?"

1 Corinthians 1:30-31 (ESV)

[30]And because of him you are in **Christ Jesus, who became to us wisdom from God**, righteousness and sanctification and redemption, [31]so that, as it is written, "Let the one who boasts, boast in the Lord."

Jesus embodies wisdom that comes exclusively from God.

3. "How are such mighty works done by his hands?"

Isaiah 9:6 (ESV)

> For to us a child is born,
> to us a son is given;
> and the government shall be upon his shoulder,
> and his name shall be called
> Wonderful Counselor, **Mighty God**,
> Everlasting Father, Prince of Peace.

It is right to call Him "Mighty God." This explains His wisdom and why He can do mighty works.

What is the Sword of the Spirit saying to we who have ears?

90
Jesus Trumps Pilate

John 19:10–11 (ESV)

[10]So Pilate said to him, "You will not speak to me? Do you not know that I have authority to release you and authority to crucify you?" [11]Jesus answered him, "You would have no authority over me at all unless it had been given you from above. Therefore he who delivered me over to you has the greater sin."

Pilate has an inflated perception of his power beyond reality. Jesus is on trial, but God's plans are still right on schedule. God gave Pilate authority for God's own purpose. Jesus chose the cross and Pilate is powerless to stop him.

What is the Sword of the Spirit saying to we who have ears?

91
Holy Vows

2 Corinthians 11:2–4 (ESV)

²For I feel a divine jealousy for you, since I betrothed you to one husband, to present you as a pure virgin to Christ. ³But I am afraid that as the serpent deceived Eve by his cunning, your thoughts will be led astray from a sincere and pure devotion to Christ. ⁴For if someone comes and proclaims another Jesus than the one we proclaimed, or if you receive a different spirit from the one you received, or if you accept a different gospel from the one you accepted, you put up with it readily enough.

Paul had visited Corinth and preached the gospel of Jesus to lost people; some of these he betrothed to Christ. Now, he's writing this difficult letter to that blood-washed and spirit-filled church at Corinth; some of whom were being tempted by false messages.

Part of the church was listening to talk of a different Jesus. Some were considering different gospels. If they continued down that road then they would be adulterers, violating the vows they took when they were joined to Jesus of Nazareth.

What is the Sword of the Spirit saying to we who have ears?

92
Kingdom Structure

Mark 6:7–13 (ESV)

⁷And he called the twelve and began to send them out two by two, and gave them authority over the unclean spirits. ⁸He charged them to take nothing for their journey except a staff—no bread, no bag, no money in their belts— ⁹but to wear sandals and not put on two tunics. ¹⁰And he said to them, "Whenever you enter a house, stay there until you depart from there. ¹¹And if any place will not receive you and they will not listen to you, when you leave, shake off the dust that is on your feet as a testimony against them." ¹²So they went out and proclaimed that people should repent. ¹³And they cast out many demons and anointed with oil many who were sick and healed them.

Jesus's authority is great. He demonstrates his authority by giving his disciples power over disease and demons, along with authority to preach the message. The theme of the message is to repent in anticipation of the coming kingdom (Mark 1:15).

Sending out the "twelve" is a powerful administrative action mirroring God's historical governance of the twelve tribes of his chosen people. God provided law to them on the mountain through his prophet Moses (Exodus 24:12). Jesus declared his right to rule when he called the twelve disciples, also on a mountain (Mark 3:13–19).

The patterns of evidence show the hand of God in both covenants.

What is the Sword of the Spirit saying to we who have ears?

🕊 93 🕊
Jesus Feeds 5000 in Exodus Style

Mark 6:34–44 (ESV)

³⁴When he went ashore he saw a great crowd, and he had compassion on them, because they were like sheep without a shepherd. And he began to teach them many things. ³⁵And when it grew late, his disciples came to him and said, "This is a desolate place, and the hour is now late. ³⁶Send them away to go into the surrounding countryside and villages and buy themselves something to eat." ³⁷But he answered them, "You give them something to eat." And they said to him, "Shall we go and buy two hundred denarii worth of bread and give it to them to eat?" ³⁸And he said to them, "How many loaves do you have? Go and see." And when they had found out, they said, "Five, and two fish." ³⁹Then he commanded them all to sit down in groups on the green grass. ⁴⁰So they sat down in groups, by hundreds and by fifties. ⁴¹And taking the five loaves and the two fish, he looked up to heaven and said a blessing and broke the loaves and gave them to the disciples to set before the people. And he divided the two fish among them all. ⁴²And they all ate and were satisfied. ⁴³And they took up twelve baskets full of broken pieces and of the fish. ⁴⁴And those who ate the loaves were five thousand men.

A multitude had followed Jesus into a "desolate place," a wilderness. It's getting late and they are getting hungry, out in the wilderness. Doesn't this setting sound familiar? It should have seemed very familiar to the Jews.

The Jews would remember the Exodus Journey.

> "But God led the people around by the way of the wilderness toward the Red Sea. And the people of Israel went up out of the land of Egypt equipped for battle." -- Exodus 13:18

The Jews would remember the wilderness teaching of God.

> "Then the Lord said to him, "Who has made man's mouth? Who makes him mute, or deaf, or seeing, or blind? Is it not I, the **Lord**? 12Now therefore go, and I will be with your mouth and teach you what you shall speak." -- Exodus 4:11–12

The Jews would remember God feeding thousands of their ancestors.

> "Then the **Lord** said to Moses, "Behold, I am about to rain bread from heaven for you, and the people shall go out and gather a day's portion every day, that I may test them, whether they will walk in my law or not." -- Exodus 16:4

God can be recognized by his works.

What is the Sword of the Spirit saying to we who have ears?

94
Divine Control

Mark 6:47–52 (ESV)

[47] And when evening came, the boat was out on the sea, and he was alone on the land. [48] And he saw that they were making headway painfully, for the wind was against them. And about the fourth watch of the night he came to them, walking on the sea. He meant to pass by them, [49] but when they saw him walking on the sea they thought it was a ghost, and cried out, [50] for they all saw him and were terrified. But immediately he spoke to them and said, "Take heart; it is I. Do not be afraid." [51] And he got into the boat with them, and the wind ceased. And they were utterly astounded, [52] for they did not understand about the loaves, but their hearts were hardened.

The storm was great, the boat was small, and the disciples were afraid. Jesus walks on water before he calms the wind and the waves.

The following Psalm praises The One who possesses such supernatural powers.

Psalm 107:28–30 (ESV)

[28] Then they cried to the LORD in their trouble,
and he delivered them from their distress.

[29] He made the storm be still,
and the waves of the sea were hushed.

[30] Then they were glad that the waters were quiet,
and he brought them to their desired haven.

Jesus' identity is revealed in the actions he took against the storm on the Sea of Galilee. It is appropriate that the disciples react with fear and amazement.

What is the Sword of the Spirit saying to we who have ears?

95
An Unusual Healing, or Not

Mark 7:31–37 (ESV)

³¹Then he returned from the region of Tyre and went through Sidon to the Sea of Galilee, in the region of the Decapolis. ³²And they brought to him a man who was deaf and had a speech impediment, and they begged him to lay his hand on him. ³³And taking him aside from the crowd privately, he put his fingers into his ears, and after spitting touched his tongue. ³⁴And looking up to heaven, he sighed and said to him, "Ephphatha," that is, "Be opened." ³⁵And his ears were opened, his tongue was released, and he spoke plainly. ³⁶And Jesus charged them to tell no one. But the more he charged them, the more zealously they proclaimed it. ³⁷And they were astonished beyond measure, saying, "He has done all things well. He even makes the deaf hear and the mute speak."

Why did Jesus use saliva and touch the tongue? Strange as it seems, it worked. It's similar to going to the manufacturer of an appliance and expecting to receive the most appropriate parts and repairs. We can have even higher expectations with Jesus because he created man.

Recall how familiar Jesus is with the process of creation.

Colossians 1:13b–17 (ESV)

[13b]His beloved Son, [14]in whom we have redemption, the forgiveness of sins. [15]He is the image of the invisible God, the firstborn of all creation. [16]For by him all things were created, in heaven and on earth, visible and invisible, whether thrones or dominions or rulers or authorities—all things were created through him and for him. [17]And he is before all things, and in him all things hold together.

We should not be surprised that the Creator is able to heal what He has created.

What is the Sword of the Spirit saying to we who have ears?

96
The Kingdom Arrived with Power

Mark 9:1 (ESV)

And he said to them, "Truly, I say to you, there are some standing here who will not taste death until they see the kingdom of God after it has come with power."

Among those standing there were eleven apostles. They would witness the powerful coming of the kingdom.

After his resurrection, Jesus repeated this promise; this was during the 40 day period in which he taught the eleven before ascending to the right hand of the Father.

Acts 1:8 (ESV)

"But you will receive power when the Holy Spirit has come upon you, and you will be my witnesses in Jerusalem and in all Judea and Samaria, and to the end of the earth."

The kingdom hadn't come just yet. The kingdom would arrive fewer than ten days after Jesus repeated this promise.

Acts 2:1–3 (ESV)

¹When the day of Pentecost arrived, they were all together in one place. ²And suddenly there came from heaven a sound like a mighty rushing wind, and it filled the entire house where they were sitting. ³And divided tongues as of fire appeared to them and rested on each one of them. ⁴And they were all filled with the Holy Spirit and began to speak in other tongues as the Spirit gave them utterance.

The Kingdom has finally arrived: with the power of mighty wind, tongues of fire, and a message of salvation in many languages. The 3,000 who were baptized (Acts 2:41) heard that message of the Kingdom of God preached with power by Holy Spirit-empowered apostles. Those 3,000 were placed in The Kingdom.

What is the Sword of the Spirit saying to we who have ears?

97
The Kingdom Now

Acts 8:12 (ESV)

But when they [the Samaritans] believed Philip as he preached good news about the kingdom of God and the name of Jesus Christ, they were baptized, both men and women.

This was no message of dreams for a Pollyanna future that must be offset with a judicious dose of cautionary doubt. This was good news of the kingdom applicable right now!

These men and women entered God's kingdom that day under the authority of King Jesus Christ. They entered it through baptism, through Christ, just as 3,000 did on the day of Pentecost (Acts 2:28-41).

What is the Sword of the Spirit saying to we who have ears?

98
Jesus Died

Jesus died; how could this have happened? Who is responsible? The Holy Spirit answers through Peter:

Acts 3:17–18 (NIV)

¹⁷"Now, fellow Israelites, I know that you acted in ignorance, as did your leaders. ¹⁸But this is how God fulfilled what he had foretold through all the prophets, saying that his Messiah would suffer.

God's plan had been declared by prophets who described the sufferings Jesus would endure. But, "Why?"

Because God fulfilled his plan that "his Messiah* would suffer." God intends Jesus's victory over sin and death to benefit all those willing to hear.

As much as they would like, neither leaders of men nor Satan can take credit for Jesus' death; only God gets the glory.

What is the Sword of the Spirit saying to we who have ears?

---

* "His Messiah," God has only one Messiah.

99
A Prophet Like Moses?

Deuteronomy 18:15–20 (ESV)

[15]"The Lord your God will raise up for you a prophet like me from among you, from your brothers—it is to him you shall listen— [16]just as you desired of the Lord your God at Horeb on the day of the assembly, when you said, 'Let me not hear again the voice of the Lord my God or see this great fire any more, lest I die.' [17]And the Lord said to me, 'They are right in what they have spoken. [18]I will raise up for them a prophet like you from among their brothers. And I will put my words in his mouth, and he shall speak to them all that I command him. [19]And whoever will not listen to my words that he shall speak in my name, I myself will require it of him. [20]But the prophet who presumes to speak a word in my name that I have not commanded him to speak, or who speaks in the name of other gods, that same prophet shall die.'"

Prophets speak for God. God told Moses that He would raise up a Moses-like prophet from among his fellow Israelites. This particular prophet must be listened to, or else there would be consequences.

Has that prophet come? If so, who is it?

Mark 9:4–8 (ESV)

⁴And there appeared to them Elijah with Moses, and they were talking with Jesus. ⁵And Peter said to Jesus, "Rabbi, it is good that we are here. Let us make three tents, one for you and one for Moses and one for Elijah." ⁶For he did not know what to say, for they were terrified. ⁷And a cloud overshadowed them, and a voice came out of the cloud, "This is my beloved Son; listen to him." ⁸And suddenly, looking around, they no longer saw anyone with them but Jesus only.

Jesus is the prophet we must listen to. We know because the Father's voice identified him from out of the cloud. We know because the Father "raised him up" from out of the grave. We know because Jesus' Apostles affirmed that Jesus was the one Moses had prophesied (Acts 3:17–26).

If we don't want to listen to Jesus, we "shall be destroyed from the people" (Acts 3:23).

What is the Sword of the Spirit saying to we who have ears?

100
A Father's Prayer

Mark 9:16–29 (ESV)

[16] And he asked them, "What are you arguing about with them?" [17] And someone from the crowd answered him, "Teacher, I brought my son to you, for he has a spirit that makes him mute. [18] And whenever it seizes him, it throws him down, and he foams and grinds his teeth and becomes rigid. So I asked your disciples to cast it out, and they were not able." [19] And he answered them, "O faithless generation, how long am I to be with you? How long am I to bear with you? Bring him to me." [20] And they brought the boy to him. And when the spirit saw him, immediately it convulsed the boy, and he fell on the ground and rolled about, foaming at the mouth. [21] And Jesus asked his father, "How long has this been happening to him?" And he said, "From childhood. [22] And it has often cast him into fire and into water, to destroy him. But if you can do anything, have compassion on us and help us." [23] And Jesus said to him, "'If you can'! All things are possible for one who believes." [24] Immediately the father of the child cried out and said, "I believe; help my unbelief!" [25] And when Jesus saw that a crowd came running together, he rebuked the unclean spirit, saying to it, "You mute and deaf spirit, I command you, come out of him and never enter him again." [26] And after crying out and convulsing him terribly, it came out, and the boy was like a corpse, so that most of them said, "He is dead." [27] But Jesus took him by the hand and lifted him up, and he arose. [28] And when he had entered the house, his disciples asked him privately, "Why could we not cast it out?" [29] And he said to them, "This kind cannot be driven out by anything but prayer."

The disciples could not cast out the unclean spirit. Prayer was necessary, and a prayer was made.

> ...The father of the child cried out and said, "I believe; help my unbelief!"

The father of the boy prayed to the right one. Jesus answered his prayer of faith with divine power.*

What is the Sword of the Spirit saying to we who have ears?

---

* The father of the boy was not the only one who prayed to Jesus. As Stephen was dying he prayed: "Lord Jesus, receive my spirit," Acts 7:59.

101
The Father's Family Planning

1 Peter 1:1–2 (ESV)

¹Peter, an apostle of Jesus Christ, To those who are elect exiles of the Dispersion in Pontus, Galatia, Cappadocia, Asia, and Bithynia, ²according to the foreknowledge of God the Father, in the sanctification of the Spirit, for obedience to Jesus Christ and for sprinkling with his blood: May grace and peace be multiplied to you.

Peter writes the church, calling them exiles.* They are exiles in this world while they anticipate reaching the heavenly home which Jesus is preparing for them.

Yes, Jesus died. But he arose from the dead, so the church obeys.

The Father, in his foreknowledge, had determined that Jesus' blood and the Spirit would sanctify† this people. That is what Jesus commanded and that is what the church obeys. His people have always entered Jesus' church by that blood and the Spirit (Acts 2:38, Acts 20:28). In the church we all are in God's family as "sons of God" (Galatians 3:25–27).

What is the Sword of the Spirit saying to we who have ears?

---

* "exiles," meaning refugees longing for their homeland.
† "Sanctify," meaning to "make holy" or "set apart for holy purpose". It can also mean to cleanse from sins (Titus 3:5).

❦ 102 ❦
Exodus, Available Only Through Jesus

Jude 1:4–5 (NIV)

⁴For certain individuals whose condemnation was written about long ago have secretly slipped in among you. They are ungodly people, who pervert the grace of our God into a license for immorality and deny Jesus Christ our only Sovereign and Lord.

⁵Though you already know all this, I want to remind you that the Lord at one time delivered his people out of Egypt, but later destroyed those who did not believe.

How many Lords are over the church? Jude and the Holy Spirit remind the church that "Jesus Christ" is "our only Sovereign and Lord;" there's none other.

Additionally, we learn of work Jesus performed during the Exodus. He delivered the Israelites out of Egypt. When some of them failed to believe, Jesus destroyed them.

This is the same Jesus who died on the cross, offering an Exodus* for all.

What is the Sword of the Spirit saying to we who have ears?

---

* In Luke 9:31 (NIV) Jesus talks with Moses and Elijah, "They spoke about his departure, which he was about to bring to fulfillment at Jerusalem." The Greek word translated here as "departure" is commonly transliterated "Exodus.".

103
Higher Aspirations

Hebrews 11:8, 12–16 (ESV)

⁸By faith Abraham obeyed when he was called to go out to a place that he was to receive as an inheritance. And he went out, not knowing where he was going. ...

¹²Therefore from one man and him as good as dead, were born descendants as many as the stars of heaven and as many as the innumerable grains of sand by the seashore.

¹³These all died in faith, not having received the things promised, but having seen them and greeted them from afar, and having acknowledged that they were strangers and exiles on the earth. ¹⁴For people who speak thus make it clear that they are seeking a homeland. ¹⁵If they had been thinking of that land from which they had gone out, they would have had opportunity to return. ¹⁶But as it is, they desire a better country, that is, a heavenly one. Therefore God is not ashamed to be called their God, for he has prepared for them a city.

God made great promises to Abraham and his children of faith. During their lifetimes, the promises were never fully received. Yet Abraham's faithful descendants never settled for an earthly substitute for God's promises and were never satisfied with a lesser country on earth.

These men and women of faith had heavenly aspirations because the God of heaven had made heavenly promises. Therefore, they lived out their fleshly lives as "strangers and exiles*" on earth, never settling.

God is still their God; they will yet receive that heavenly city which he has prepared for them.

What is the Sword of the Spirit saying to we who have ears?

---

* "exiles" or "pilgrims." Defined in Strongs (from G3844 and the base of G1927) an alien living alongside, i.e., a resident foreigner: -- pilgrim, stranger.

104
One Is Enough

1 Timothy 2:5 (ESV)

For there is one God, and there is one mediator between God and men, the man Christ Jesus.

Suppose that someone suggests we need an additional mediator between God and Man. She might be thinking that Jesus' work only went so far, not solving enough of mankind's problems. Some have even gone so far as to say we need more Christs.

1 John 2:22-23 (ESV)

²²Who is the liar but he who denies that Jesus is the Christ? This is the antichrist, he who denies the Father and the Son. ²³No one who denies the Son has the Father; whoever acknowledges the Son has the Father also.

Jesus is "the" Christ; there are not multiple "Christs." To say that the Jesus proclaimed by the Apostles is merely "a christ" (one among many), is to deny the Father and The Son.

What is the Sword of the Spirit saying to we who have ears?

105
Longing for the Homeland

Hebrews 11:12–16 (NASB95)

¹²Therefore there was born even of one man [*Abraham*], and him as good as dead at that, as many descendants AS THE STARS OF HEAVEN IN NUMBER, AND INNUMERABLE AS THE SAND WHICH IS BY THE SEASHORE.

¹³All these died in faith, without receiving the promises, but having seen them and having welcomed them from a distance, and having confessed that they were strangers and exiles on the earth. ¹⁴For those who say such things make it clear that they are seeking a country of their own. ¹⁵And indeed if they had been thinking of that country from which they went out, they would have had opportunity to return. ¹⁶But as it is, they desire a better country, that is, a heavenly one. Therefore God is not ashamed to be called their God; for He has prepared a city for them.

"Times are bad." That would be true regardless of which decade or century in which the words are spoken. So much personal anxiety and human conflict revolves around how to fix bad times: injustice, poverty, war, prejudice, greed, etc.

People want these earthly problems solved. If they can be solved with the "kingdom of God," so much the better. That's why many put a lot of energy into reinterpreting these promises given to Abraham. They want them applied to this world and this life.

The faithful don't settle for an earthly homeland. They await the heavenly city promised by the God of heaven. They know that the God of heaven delivers!

What is the Sword of the Spirit saying to we who have ears?

106
With What Did the Master Pay?

2 Peter 2:1 (ESV)

But false prophets also arose among the people, just as there will be false teachers among you, who will secretly bring in destructive heresies, even denying the Master who bought them, bringing upon themselves swift destruction.

Peter writes to the church reminding them how valuable they are and how much the Master paid for them. He doesn't need to spell out the price, they will remember the famously high price. That's not something to throw away lightly.

Acts 20:28 (ESV)

Pay careful attention to yourselves and to all the flock, in which the Holy Spirit has made you overseers, to care for the church of God, which he obtained with his own blood.

God paid with his own blood—that is one expensive church!

The false prophets who deny the divinity of Jesus envision sin to be some sort of low hurdle, preventing entry into heaven. But their "cheap grace" proposals do not align with the price God paid.

What is the Sword of the Spirit saying to we who have ears?

107
Undivided Loyalty

Matthew 4:10 (NASB95)

Then Jesus said to him, "Go, Satan! For it is written, 'You shall worship the Lord your God, and serve Him only.'"

Matthew 6:24 (NASB95)

"No one can serve two masters; for either he will hate the one and love the other, or he will be devoted to one and despise the other. You cannot serve God and wealth.

John 13:13 (NASB95)

You call Me Teacher and Lord; and you are right, for so I am.

Serving the Lord Jesus does not cause confusion, for He is the Christian's only Lord and Master. Christians serve him and look for no other Messiah.

Who is the Lord? Jesus says that he is; he says that it is right to call him Lord. Now it is clear whom we must worship and serve.

What is the Sword of the Spirit saying to we who have ears?

108
Be All That You Can Be!

Colossians 2:8–12 (NASB95)

⁸See to it that no one takes you captive through philosophy and empty deception, according to the tradition of men, according to the elementary principles of the world, rather than according to Christ. ⁹For in Him all the fullness of Deity dwells in bodily form, ¹⁰and in Him you have been made complete, and He is the head over all rule and authority; ¹¹and in Him you were also circumcised with a circumcision made without hands, in the removal of the body of the flesh by the circumcision of Christ; ¹²having been buried with Him in baptism, in which you were also raised up with Him through faith in the working of God, who raised Him from the dead.

Sinners, have hope! In Jesus can be found all that you lack.

Christians are sinners who have entered into Jesus Christ. In Jesus they receive all that they had been missing—when they were on the outside looking in. Jesus is where it's at, where "all the fullness of Deity dwells."

What is the Sword of the Spirit saying to we who have ears?

109
The Mystery Revealed

2 Corinthians 3:14 (ESV)

> But their minds were hardened. For to this day, when they read the old covenant, that same veil remains unlifted, because only through Christ is it taken away.

There really are mysteries hidden within the Old Covenant scriptures. For ages, these truths from the Spirit remain veiled within Moses, The Writings, and The Prophets.

These mysteries will not be understood through diligent study. Searching for patterns will fail, whether the pattern is of history or scripture.

Only through Christ is the mystery revealed.

What is the Sword of the Spirit saying to we who have ears?

❦ 110 ❦
The Church: Valued and Cared For

Acts 20:28 (ESV)

Pay careful attention to yourselves and to all the flock, in which the Holy Spirit has made you overseers, to care for the church of God, which he obtained with his own blood.

God places a high value on the church. We must make sure to be part of the blood-bought church, which God values so highly. I can't possibly imagine I can please God while refusing his invitation into his church.*

God also cares for the church by providing overseers† (elders) who act as shepherds.

What is the Sword of the Spirit saying to we who have ears?

---

* Many directly refuse the invitation into the church, but some try to modify the conditions. The invitation into the church is the gospel, which has conditions. Jesus told a parable of a King who invited many to the wedding of his son. But there was one man who wanted to be there on his own terms; he did not arrive in the expected wedding clothes. Jesus describes the king's reaction, "He asked, 'How did you get in here without wedding clothes, friend?' The man was speechless. Then the king told the attendants, 'Tie him hand and foot, and throw him outside, into the darkness, where there will be weeping and gnashing of teeth.'" (Matthew 22:12-13)

† The apostle Paul is addressing his words to the overseers of the church at Ephesus here in Acts 20:28. Through Paul, the Holy Spirit is giving them instructions before Paul travels to Jerusalem.

111
Get In Your Right Mind

Philippians 2:5–8 (ESV)

⁵Have this mind among yourselves, which is yours in Christ Jesus, ⁶who, though he was in the form of God, did not count equality with God a thing to be grasped, ⁷but emptied himself, by taking the form of a servant, being born in the likeness of men. ⁸And being found in human form, he humbled himself by becoming obedient to the point of death, even death on a cross.

Self-preservation is a basic instinct of all flesh. When one needlessly puts himself, and others, at risk we use this expression, "He's out of his mind!"

Jesus' mind did not focus on fleshly solutions ("All flesh is like grass,"*). The mind of Jesus was Spiritual ("the desires of the Spirit are against the flesh,"†), He humbled Himself in obedience to the Father's will,‡ our highest purpose.

---

* 1 Peter 1:24-25 (ESV) "for 'All flesh is like grass and all its glory like the flower of grass. The grass withers, and the flower falls, but the word of the Lord remains forever.'"
† Galatians 5:17 (ESV) "For the desires of the flesh are against the Spirit, and the desires of the Spirit are against the flesh, for these are opposed to each other, to keep you from doing the things you want to do."
‡ Matthew 26:39 (ESV) "And going a little farther he fell on his face and prayed, saying, 'My Father, if it be possible, let this cup pass from me; nevertheless, not as I will, but as you will.'"

Jesus is the King of the universe who turned the world upside down.* We need to have His mind. Don't fear being called "out of your mind," when walking in His steps.

What is the Sword of the Spirit saying to we who have ears?

---

* Acts 17:6 (ESV) "...These men who have turned the world upside down have come here also,..."

✦ 112 ✦
The King to Top All Kings!

1 Timothy 6:13–16 (ESV)

¹³I charge you in the presence of God, who gives life to all things, and of Christ Jesus, who in his testimony before Pontius Pilate made the good confession, ¹⁴to keep the commandment unstained and free from reproach until the appearing of our Lord Jesus Christ, ¹⁵which he will display at the proper time—he who is the blessed and only Sovereign, the King of kings and Lord of lords, ¹⁶who alone has immortality, who dwells in unapproachable light, whom no one has ever seen or can see. To him be honor and eternal dominion. Amen.

Jesus is going to appear, which is quite awesome since there is so much chaos going on, so much lawlessness.

But not all are willing to bow to Jesus, to accept what he's done, to accept his rule. Some have gone so far as to invent a different Jesus for their imagined future; that's because their eyes are closed to the real Jesus.

The real Jesus is one who made the "good confession" before "Pontius Pilate" (Mark 15:2). He confessed that he's the king of the Jews, that he's the king of salvation,* and that he's the king of judgment day.†

Don't go looking elsewhere for a king. The crucified Jesus is the "only Sovereign," now reigning in hearts near you.

What is the Sword of the Spirit saying to we who have ears?

---

* He's the king of an eternal kingdom. "Therefore let us be grateful for receiving a kingdom that cannot be shaken…" Hebrews 12:28 (ESV)

† King Jesus is also the judgment day judge. "And hath given him authority to execute judgment also, because he is the Son of man" John 5:27 (KJV). "For we must all appear before the judgment seat of Christ, so that each one may receive what is due for what he has done in the body, whether good or evil" 2 Corinthians 5:10 (ESV).

113
Christians Looking Up To …

Philippians 3:13–14 (ESV)

> Brothers, I do not consider that I have made it my own. But one thing I do: forgetting what lies behind and straining forward to what lies ahead, I press on toward the goal for the prize of the upward call of God in Christ Jesus.

Paul writes to the Christians in Philippi, reminding them of their goal. Their goal is upward. Jesus reigns in heaven and Christians are going to meet him.

God set forth a goal that is not earthly. So don't be looking down. This world is passing away. Therefore, Christians look forward to being "caught up together with them in the clouds to meet the Lord in the air, and so we will always be with the Lord" (1 Thessalonians 4:17).

Earthly Kingdom? No, "our citizenship is in heaven" (Philippians 3:20).

What is the Sword of the Spirit saying to we who have ears?

114
God Fully Meets Our Needs

Philippians 4:19 (ESV)

And my God will supply every need of yours according to his riches in glory in Christ Jesus.

As sinners, our needs are infinite.

Matthew 25:46 (ESV)

And these will go away into eternal punishment, but the righteous into eternal life.

Having sinned against the infinite God, we face an eternal punishment. This requires an infinitely effective solution.

But the Christians in Philippi are covered; their infinite need for salvation is supplied by being in the infinite Christ Jesus. His blood continually cleanses them from all sin.* Not only their sins, but ours too can be cleansed by Christ.

What is the Sword of the Spirit saying to we who have ears?

---

* "But if we walk in the light, as he is in the light, we have fellowship with one another, and the blood of Jesus his Son cleanses us from all sin," 1 John 1:7 (ESV)

❦ 115 ❦
Don't Fight the Cross

Philippians 3:18–21 (NIV)

¹⁸For, as I have often told you before and now tell you again even with tears, many live as enemies of the cross of Christ. ¹⁹Their destiny is destruction, their god is their stomach, and their glory is in their shame. Their mind is set on earthly things. ²⁰But our citizenship is in heaven. And we eagerly await a Savior from there, the Lord Jesus Christ, ²¹who, by the power that enables him to bring everything under his control, will transform our lowly bodies so that they will be like his glorious body.

Setting one's mind on earthly things puts one at war with the God of heaven.*

When I was in my elementary school years, I heard about the crucifixion of Jesus. Naturally, I was horrified. I imagined myself being there and rescuing Jesus from this fate. I envisioned using a military group equipped with tanks and bazookas, "that should save Jesus!" But my thoughts were earthly; I was fighting Christ.

---

* James 4:4 (ESV) "You adulterous people! Do you not know that friendship with the world is enmity with God? Therefore whoever wishes to be a friend of the world makes himself an enemy of God."

It was Christ's cross, not the Judeans', not Herod's, and not Pilate's

1 Corinthians 1:18 (NIV)

For the message of the cross is foolishness to those who are perishing, but to us who are being saved it is the power of God.

I was foolish, in my elementary school way of thinking. The cross is God's chosen power tool for salvation.

What is the Sword of the Spirit saying to we who have ears?

116
Meet God's Gift

Ephesians 2:8-9 (ESV)

⁸For by grace you have been saved through faith. And this is not your own doing; it is the gift of God, ⁹not a result of works, so that no one may boast.

A gift is something given willingly. A gift is not something we deserve. We do not bargain with the giver for our gift.

If we could have forced God to save us (how absurd), then the salvation was not by grace. If we deserved salvation, then we didn't need God's gift in the first place. If we cut a deal with God, then it was our work and not a gift.

John 3:16 (ESV)

"For God so loved the world, that he gave his only Son, that whoever believes in him should not perish but have eternal life."

We did not trick God. God was not coerced. God loved and God gave. Meet His gift and get to know Him.

What is the Sword of the Spirit saying to we who have ears?

117
The Origins of Mankind

1 Corinthians 8:4–6 (NIV)

⁴So then, about eating food sacrificed to idols: We know that "An idol is nothing at all in the world" and that "There is no God but one." ⁵For even if there are so-called gods, whether in heaven or on earth (as indeed there are many "gods" and many "lords"), ⁶yet for us there is but one God, the Father, from whom all things came and for whom we live; and there is but one Lord, Jesus Christ, through whom all things came and through whom we live.

Mankind came from God the Father through only one Lord: that being Jesus Christ.

We are not dealing with an ancient philosopher. Without Jesus, there is no Adam. Without Jesus, there would not even be a "us," you the reader and I the writer.

What is the Sword of the Spirit saying to we who have ears?

118
Where Did God Come From?

Romans 9:4–5 (ESV)

> They are Israelites, and to them belong the adoption, the glory, the covenants, the giving of the law, the worship, and the promises. To them belong the patriarchs, and from their race, according to the flesh, is the Christ, who is God over all, blessed forever. Amen.

Many people want to know where God came from. The answer is "nowhere." That's because God has always been; this is affirmed by God's unchanging nature.*

In what sense does the Holy Spirit say that Christ "is God over all?" In the same sense that the Father is eternally unchanging, so Christ is eternally unchanging.† In the same way, we must acknowledge that Jesus created all things.‡

---

* "They will perish, but you will remain; they will all wear out like a garment. You will change them like a robe, and they will pass away, but you are the same, and your years have no end" Psalm 102:26-27 (ESV).
† "Jesus Christ is the same yesterday and today and forever" Hebrews 13:8 (ESV).
‡ "He is the image of the invisible God, the firstborn of all creation. For by him all things were created, in heaven and on earth, visible and invisible, whether thrones or dominions or rulers or authorities—all things were created through him and for him. And he is before all things, and in him all things hold together" Colossians 1:15-17 (ESV).

In just one limited sense, "according to the flesh," we can say where God came from. "According to the flesh," God came from the Israelites. Jesus chose, before the creation of the world, to be born of an Israelite named Mary.

What is the Sword of the Spirit saying to we who have ears?

❦ 119 ❦
Jesus: Invisible Once Again

1 Timothy 6:13–16 (ESV)

¹³I charge you in the presence of God, who gives life to all things, and of Christ Jesus, who in his testimony before Pontius Pilate made the good confession, ¹⁴to keep the commandment unstained and free from reproach until the appearing of our Lord Jesus Christ, ¹⁵which he will display at the proper time—he who is the blessed and only Sovereign, the King of kings and Lord of lords, ¹⁶who alone has immortality, who dwells in unapproachable light, whom no one has ever seen or can see. To him be honor and eternal dominion. Amen.

When Jesus emptied himself,* he was The Word becoming flesh.† That's the invisible, becoming visible. For a Jew this is truly unexpected. It would be startling because they recall how God responded to Moses' request to see God's glory‡. God exists within "unapproachable light."

---

* "Have this mind among yourselves, which is yours in Christ Jesus, 6 who, though he was in the form of God, did not count equality with God a thing to be grasped, 7 but emptied himself, by taking the form of a servant, being born in the likeness of men. The form of God is invisible; Jesus took on visibility when he deigned to be born in the likeness of men" Philippians 2:5-7 (ESV).

† "In the beginning was the Word, and the Word was with God, and the Word was God" John 1:1 (ESV). "And the Word became flesh and dwelt among us, and we have seen his glory, glory as of the only Son from the Father, full of grace and truth" John 1:14 (ESV). Through the apostle John, the Holy Spirit talks about Jesus as the eternal "Word." The "Word" is clearly stated to be God who then becomes flesh

‡ "'Then Moses said, 'Now show me your glory'" Exodus 33:18 (ESV). "'But,' he said, 'you cannot see my face, for man shall not see me and live'" Exodus 33:20 (ESV).

After Jesus' ascension from the earth, people no longer witnessed him in the flesh. The Word returned to heaven , in unapproachable light. So Saul of Tarsus never saw Jesus during his encounter on the road to Damascus; he only saw a blinding light. This trip was after Jesus' ascension.

John 17:5 (ESV)

And now, Father, glorify me in your own presence with the glory that I had with you before the world existed.

Jesus shared the glory. He created the world and entered into it, leaving that glory for a time. Now, having ascended to heaven, that eternal glory is Jesus' once again.

Jesus is now gloriously invisible, as it should be.

What is the Sword of the Spirit saying to we who have ears?

120
Empowered to Switch Dominions

Acts 26:15–18 (NASB95)

¹⁵And I [Paul] said, 'Who are You, Lord?' And the Lord said, 'I am Jesus whom you are persecuting. ¹⁶But get up and stand on your feet; for this purpose I have appeared to you, to appoint you a minister and a witness not only to the things which you have seen, but also to the things in which I will appear to you; ¹⁷rescuing you from the Jewish people and from the Gentiles, to whom I am sending you, ¹⁸to open their eyes so that they may turn from darkness to light and from the dominion of Satan to God, that they may receive forgiveness of sins and an inheritance among those who have been sanctified by faith in Me.'

Paul was relating the commission Jesus gave him (given while he was still known as "Saul of Tarsus"). Paul was commanded to provide an enlightening message that offers people a choice.

Paul offers his hearers God's grace through Jesus—should they so choose. If Paul's hearers choose faith in Jesus, fabulous blessings result. They leave Satan's destructive dominion and enter into God's blessed kingdom. They leave off being slaves under Satan's rule and become children of God. The family aspect of God's dominion is indicated by the receipt of an inheritance along with forgiveness.

This message Paul shared is the same good news proclaimed by all the Apostles; it's the gospel of Jesus Christ. Jesus commanded this gospel to be preached by Saul of Tarsus just as the other Apostles had been commanded* to preach.

Jesus is fully in charge of His Kingdom; He won't be relinquishing His kingdom to any Johnny-come-lately.† It's Jesus' gospel. It's faith in Jesus.

Switch to God's dominion before Jesus' offer expires.

What is the Sword of the Spirit saying to we who have ears?

---

* "And Jesus came up and spoke to them, saying, "All authority has been given to Me in heaven and on earth. Go therefore and make disciples of all the nations, baptizing them in the name of the Father and the Son and the Holy Spirit, teaching them to observe all that I commanded you; and lo, I am with you always, even to the end of the age" Matthew 28:18-20 (NASB95).

† "...then comes the end, when He hands over the kingdom to the God and Father, when He has abolished all rule and all authority and power" 1 Corinthians 15:24 (NASB95).

121
Flesh Won't Make the Cut

1 Corinthians 15:50 (ESV)

I tell you this, brothers: flesh and blood cannot inherit the kingdom of God, nor does the perishable inherit the imperishable.

Day in and day out we find that earthly troubles and annoyances hurt us and bother us. They distract and tempt us to take our eyes off of Jesus and the Spiritual Kingdom. We will fall for the Devil's trick if he can get us to seek a fleshly kingdom, an earthly, perishable one. He wants us to doubt God's promises and Jesus' power to fulfill them.

But Christians are Spiritual, "born of the Spirit".* We worship a God who is Spirit.†

1 Corinthians 15:23–25 (ESV)

But each in his own order: Christ the firstfruits, then at his coming those who belong to Christ. Then comes the end, when he delivers the kingdom to God the Father after destroying every rule and every authority and power. For he must reign until he has put all his enemies under his feet.

---

*   "Jesus answered, "Truly, truly, I say to you, unless one is born of water and the Spirit, he cannot enter the kingdom of God" John 3:5 (ESV).
†   "God is spirit, and those who worship him must worship in spirit and truth" John 4:24 (ESV).

Christians are in the Kingdom. What will happen to them? Jesus will deliver them to His Father.

Some get confused about how Jesus can do this—Jesus makes it clear that "the kingdom of God" is His kingdom.* So, He can do with it as He pleases because He is God.

What is the Sword of the Spirit saying to we who have ears?

---

* "For in this way there will be richly provided for you an entrance into the eternal kingdom of our Lord and Savior Jesus Christ. Jesus' kingdom is eternally His kingdom." 2 Peter 1:11 (ESV).

122
Royal Promises, and Divine

1 Chronicles 17:11–14 (ESV)

¹¹When your days are fulfilled to walk with your fathers, I will raise up your offspring after you, one of your own sons, and I will establish his kingdom. ¹²He shall build a house for me, and I will establish his throne forever. ¹³I will be to him a father, and he shall be to me a son. I will not take my steadfast love from him, as I took it from him who was before you, ¹⁴but I will confirm him in my house and in my kingdom forever, and his throne shall be established forever.'"

Thus God speaks great promises to King David concerning his offspring. Who could God have in mind to fulfill these tremendous blessings? I must admit that David's son Solomon has often come to my mind when trying to visualize how God fulfilled these promises. But as I read this passage more carefully, Solomon does not fit. Solomon did not fulfill all these promises. The most glaring failure is that Solomon is dead, thus he is not confirmed in God's house and kingdom eternally; Solomon has left the throne.

Only an eternal king, a divine king, could fulfill such promises as God made to David. Jesus fulfilled them all; Jesus is God.

- Jesus is an offspring of David through Mary*
- Jesus built a house for God†
- Jesus was the only begotten son of the Father‡
- The Father's steadfast love never left Jesus (He never sinned)§
- Jesus reigns in God's house (the church¶) and the kingdom forever and ever**

What is the Sword of the Spirit saying to we who have ears?

---

* See Mary's Genalogy through her father Heli in Luke 3:23-38. David is listed as her ancestor in Luke 3:31.

† "Jesus answered them, 'Destroy this temple, and in three days I will raise it up.' The Jews then said, 'It has taken forty-six years to build this temple, and will you raise it up in three days?' But he was speaking about the temple of his body." John 2:19-21 (ESV).

‡ "For God so loved the world, that He gave His only begotten Son, that whoever believes in Him shall not perish, but have eternal life" John 3:16 (NASB95).

§ "The Father loves the Son and has given all things into his hand" John 3:35 (ESV). Hebrews 4:15 (ESV) For we do not have a high priest who is unable to sympathize with our weaknesses, but one who in every respect has been tempted as we are, yet without sin.

¶ "And he put all things under his feet and gave him as head over all things to the church, which is his body, the fullness of him who fills all in all" Ephesians 1:22-23 (ESV).

** "For in this way there will be richly provided for you an entrance into the eternal kingdom of our Lord and Savior Jesus Christ" 2 Peter 1:11 (ESV).
"and made us a kingdom, priests to his God and Father, to him be glory and dominion forever and ever. Amen" Revelation 1:6 (ESV).

❧ 123 ❧
A Good Word from Jesus' Blood

Hebrews 12:22–24 (NIV)

But you have come to Mount Zion, to the city of the living God, the heavenly Jerusalem. You have come to thousands upon thousands of angels in joyful assembly, to the church of the firstborn, whose names are written in heaven. You have come to God, the Judge of all, to the spirits of the righteous made perfect, to Jesus the mediator of a new covenant, and to the sprinkled blood that speaks a better word than the blood of Abel.

Genesis 4:10 (ESV)

And the Lord said, "What have you done? The voice of your brother's blood is crying to me from the ground.

Permit me to play Devil's advocate for a moment. Suppose we say that the sprinkled blood of Jesus does not speak a better word than that of Abel. The blood of Abel spoke, "Cain is Guilty," and "Cain deserves to die." We would all agree that these are bad words. The Devil might argue, "Shouldn't the death of a sinless Jesus be even worse than the death of Abel, someone who had sinned?" Following his logic, the blood of Jesus speaks an even worse cry, "Unimaginably guilty!", or possibly "You are more deserving of Hell!" The crime could also be considered worse because Jesus is God's only begotten son, whereas Abel was merely a man.

However, the Holy Spirit contradicts the Devil, saying that Jesus' blood "speaks a better word than the blood of Abel." Listen to the good sound of Jesus' blood:

Revelation 1:4–6 (ESV)

> John to the seven churches that are in Asia: Grace to you and peace from him who is and who was and who is to come, and from the seven spirits who are before his throne, and from Jesus Christ the faithful witness, the firstborn of the dead, and the ruler of kings on earth. To him who loves us and has freed us from our sins by his blood and made us a kingdom, priests to his God and Father, to him be glory and dominion forever and ever. Amen.

His blood speaks of Jesus' love. His blood proclaims deliverance from slavery to sin. His blood can bring us into His kingdom as priests. The voice of Jesus' blood is sweet, if we listen.

What is the Sword of the Spirit saying to we who have ears?

124
Before Day #1

Hebrews 1:8–12 (ESV)

But of the Son he says,

> "Your throne, O God, is forever and ever,
>   the scepter of uprightness is the scepter of your kingdom.
> You have loved righteousness and hated wickedness;
>   therefore God, your God, has anointed you with the
>   oil of gladness beyond your companions." *[Psalm 45:6-7]*

And,

> "You, Lord, laid the foundation of the earth in the beginning,
>   and the heavens are the work of your hands;
> they will perish, but you remain;
>   they will all wear out like a garment,
> like a robe you will roll them up,
>   like a garment they will be changed.
> But you are the same,
>   and your years will have no end. *[Psalm 102:25-27]*

Before the first day, what was Jesus like? To put it another way, what was Jesus doing before the first day of creation?

These verses teach us a lot about Jesus. Unlike the temporary heavens and earth, Jesus remains the same. So Jesus has been on His throne before the first day of creation. During creation, our Lord Jesus laid the foundation of the earth and created the heavens. After creation, He continues to be on his throne forever, since His years have no end.

We learn that Jesus is God ("But of the Son he says, 'Your throne, O God, is forever and ever,...'").

What is the Sword of the Spirit saying to we who have ears?

125
Don't Squelch the Good News!

Romans 1:15–18 (ESV)

¹⁵So I am eager to preach the gospel to you also who are in Rome. ¹⁶For I am not ashamed of the gospel, for it is the power of God for salvation to everyone who believes, to the Jew first and also to the Greek. ¹⁷For in it the righteousness of God is revealed from faith for faith, as it is written, "The righteous shall live by faith." ¹⁸For the wrath of God is revealed from heaven against all ungodliness and unrighteousness of men, who by their unrighteousness suppress the truth.

Some people try to hide the cross. What's to be ashamed of? Yes, there was an execution involved; some might find that unpleasant. But they completely miss God's point.

The gospel ("good news") always has the cross in it. Those who drop it are left with nothing but bad news. Without the cross, the coming judgment will still apply to all mankind.

Paul is so excited about the cross, so eager to share the gospel, because it matters. Paul doesn't sugarcoat the cross—it's God's power over sin and death. It's the truth.

If preached, the cross matters. When the preaching is heard, it can be believed. When believed, God saves.

If the cross is suppressed, God will direct his wrath upon those who are hiding the truth.

1 Corinthians 1:18 (ESV)

For the word of the cross is folly to those who are perishing, but to us who are being saved it is the power of God.

What is the Sword of the Spirit saying to we who have ears?

126
Jesus Enters Both High and Humble

Mark 11:7–10 (ESV)

⁷And they brought the colt to Jesus and threw their cloaks on it, and he sat on it. ⁸And many spread their cloaks on the road, and others spread leafy branches that they had cut from the fields. ⁹And those who went before and those who followed were shouting, "Hosanna! Blessed is he who comes in the name of the Lord! ¹⁰Blessed is the coming kingdom of our father David! Hosanna in the highest!"

Jesus had instructed his disciples to procure this colt for him to make a triumphal entry into Jerusalem. He knew that this would make a stir. The colt of the donkey would be recognized as the animal on which the coming messiah would ride. In this action He claims the throne; He is the king.

Zechariah 9:9 (ESV)

Rejoice greatly, O daughter of Zion! Shout aloud, O daughter of Jerusalem! Behold, your king is coming to you; righteous and having salvation is he, humble and mounted on a donkey, on a colt, the foal of a donkey.

Psalm 118:25–26 (ESV)

²⁵Save us, we pray, O Lord! O Lord, we pray, give us success! ²⁶Blessed is he who comes in the name of the Lord! We bless you from the house of the Lord.

They cry out in Hebrew "Hosanna," meaning "Save us, we pray." This is a prayer to the Lord [Yahweh]. Jesus, most certainly, "comes in the name of the Lord!" Jesus' very name means "Yahweh Saves." The crowd recognizes God's savior-king, though the plan of salvation remains hidden.

Praise the Lord, that Jesus also came in humility, mounted on a donkey. Thank you, Jesus, for offering salvation that we do not deserve. Thank you for providing a way out of the condemnation that we clearly deserve.

What is the Sword of the Spirit saying to we who have ears?

127
The Command of the Cross

Philippians 2:5–8 (ESV)

⁵Have this mind among yourselves, which is yours in Christ Jesus, ⁶who, though he was in the form of God, did not count equality with God a thing to be grasped, ⁷but emptied himself, by taking the form of a servant, being born in the likeness of men. ⁸And being found in human form, he humbled himself by becoming obedient to the point of death, even death on a cross.

Jesus obeyed a command to die on the cross? But who commanded him?

John 14:31 (ESV)

But I do as the Father has commanded me, so that the world may know that I love the Father. Rise, let us go from here.

The Father commanded Jesus, and the Father loves Him for it.

John 10:17 (ESV)

For this reason the Father loves me, because I lay down my life that I may take it up again.

Did Jesus have a choice? Yes! As God he chose what this mission required: emptying himself into human form.

What is the Sword of the Spirit saying to we who have ears?

128
Get the Last-Days Message

Hebrews 1:1–2 (NASB95)

> God, after He spoke long ago to the fathers in the prophets in many portions and in many ways, in these last days has spoken to us in His Son, whom He appointed heir of all things, through whom also He made the world.

These are the last days. There are no more days beyond these. And this final era (these last days) is marked by God speaking to us in His Son.

God does not speak to us in His sons (plural); He has only one Son (singular) through whom he will be speaking. To some, these 2,000 years long "last days" seem very long, but God wants the message of His Son heard. Be thankful His patience determined that this loving message will continue to the end.

We can't look to fathers to listen to. We can't seek out prophets to follow. This last and final message is through God's only begotten Son.[*] Given that the Son is also our creator, His message meets our needs with all authority, all power, all love, and for all eternity.

What is the Sword of the Spirit saying to we who have ears?

---

[*] 1 John 4:9 (NASB95) – By this the love of God was manifested in us, that God has sent **His only begotten Son** into the world so that we might live through Him.

129
The Gospel in a Flask

Mark 14:3–9 (RSV)

³And while he was at Bethany in the house of Simon the leper, as he sat at table, a woman came with an alabaster flask of ointment of pure nard, very costly, and she broke the flask and poured it over his head. ⁴But there were some who said to themselves indignantly, "Why was the ointment thus wasted? ⁵For this ointment might have been sold for more than three hundred denarii, and given to the poor." And they reproached her. ⁶But Jesus said, "Let her alone; why do you trouble her? She has done a beautiful thing to me. ⁷For you always have the poor with you, and whenever you will, you can do good to them; but you will not always have me. ⁸She has done what she could; she has anointed my body beforehand for burying. ⁹And truly, I say to you, wherever the gospel is preached in the whole world, what she has done will be told in memory of her."

The Gospel had to be preached to the whole world, and would be. In that magnificent message, there is room to recount the actions of this woman. How does she fit in?

Her actions are a way to outline the Gospel. Jesus was about to be buried, upon completion of His crucifixion. His burial would be in a hurry, thus "she has anointed my body beforehand."

Jesus is worthy of all that she could indicate by anointing Him:

- Sorrow, that her sins, and ours, necessitate His death
- Gratitude, that He willingly sacrifices His life
- Honor, that the King of kings and Lord of lords overcomes death

Jesus declares the "Gospel" to include His death; otherwise, it could not be "Good News." The Gospel is worth preaching to "the whole world" because it includes both His death and His resurrection.

What is the Sword of the Spirit saying to we who have ears?

130
The Command of the Eternal God

Romans 16:25–27 (ESV)

²⁵Now to him who is able to strengthen you according to my gospel and the preaching of Jesus Christ, according to the revelation of the mystery that was kept secret for long ages ²⁶but has now been disclosed and through the prophetic writings has been made known to all nations, according to the command of the eternal God, to bring about the obedience of faith— ²⁷to the only wise God be glory forevermore through Jesus Christ! Amen.

The mystery was kept secret for long ages, in spite of the fact that it is contained in writings shared for long ages. The mystery was contained in the prophetic writings of the Jews.

What an honor it was for the Israelites to preserve the prophetic writings which God would use to bless all nations! Except for these writings, no one would have a basis for faith in Jesus Christ.

These writings contain God's promise to provide his only Son as the sacrifice for the sin of mankind.* They describe that His death was no accident, that it was God's will† to put him to death. And these writings reveal that the Son himself would be offering‡ up his life for the guilt of others.

Through these writings, the mystery is made known. Now, all nations have reason to respond in the obedience of faith.§ This is the command of the eternal God.

What is the Sword of the Spirit saying to we who have ears?

---

* Genesis 22:8 (ESV) Abraham said, "God will provide for himself the lamb for a burnt offering, my son." So they went both of them together.
† Isaiah 53:10a (ESV) Yet it was the will of the Lord to crush him; he has put him to grief...
‡ Isaiah 53:10b (ESV) ...when his soul makes an offering for guilt, he shall see his offspring; he shall prolong his days; the will of the Lord shall prosper in his hand.
§ Galatians 3:26-27 (ESV) for in Christ Jesus you are all sons of God, through faith. For as many of you as were baptized into Christ have put on Christ.

131
Jesus' Way

2 Corinthians 4:1–6 (NIV)

¹Therefore, since through God's mercy we have this ministry, we do not lose heart. ²Rather, we have renounced secret and shameful ways; we do not use deception, nor do we distort the word of God. On the contrary, by setting forth the truth plainly we commend ourselves to everyone's conscience in the sight of God. ³And even if our gospel is veiled, it is veiled to those who are perishing. ⁴The god of this age has blinded the minds of unbelievers, so that they cannot see the light of the gospel that displays the glory of Christ, who is the image of God. ⁵For what we preach is not ourselves, but Jesus Christ as Lord, and ourselves as your servants for Jesus's sake. ⁶For God, who said, "Let light shine out of darkness," made his light shine in our hearts to give us the light of the knowledge of God's glory displayed in the face of Christ.

The light of the world* did not promote Himself with tricks, deception, or lies. Jesus is also the way, the truth, and the life;† this leaves no room for falsehood. He also expects His servants to be straight forward, without using underhanded ways, without altering God's word.

---

* John 8:12 (ESV) Again Jesus spoke to them, saying, "I am the light of the world. Whoever follows me will not walk in darkness, but will have the light of life."

† John 14:6 (ESV) Jesus said to him, "I am the way, and the truth, and the life. No one comes to the Father except through me.

Satan's way is paved with lies.* Jesus way is truth. The Lord Jesus Christ is not acting when His face displays the glory of God.†

What is the Sword of the Spirit saying to we who have ears?

---

* John 8:44 (ESV) You are of your father the devil, and your will is to do your father's desires. He was a murderer from the beginning, and does not stand in the truth, because there is no truth in him. When he lies, he speaks out of his own character, for he is a liar and the father of lies.

† Acts 26:13,15 (ESV) At midday, O king, I saw on the way a light from heaven, brighter than the sun, that shone around me and those who journeyed with me. ... And I said, 'Who are you, Lord?' And the Lord said, 'I am Jesus whom you are persecuting.

☙ 132 ❧
A Death of First Importance

1 Corinthians 15:1–9 (NASB95)

¹Now I make known to you, brethren, the gospel which I preached to you, which also you received, in which also you stand, ²by which also you are saved, if you hold fast the word which I preached to you, unless you believed in vain. ³For I delivered to you as of first importance what I also received, that Christ died for our sins according to the Scriptures, ⁴and that He was buried, and that He was raised on the third day according to the Scriptures, ⁵and that He appeared to Cephas, then to the twelve. ⁶After that He appeared to more than five hundred brethren at one time, most of whom remain until now, but some have fallen asleep; ⁷then He appeared to James, then to all the apostles; ⁸and last of all, as to one untimely born, He appeared to me also. ⁹For I am the least of the apostles, and not fit to be called an apostle, because I persecuted the church of God.

Paul is recounting to these Christians the gospel. They had received it from Paul. It's the good news by which they are being saved.

What is of first importance? It's the whole gospel that Paul received from God. Paul then lists essential gospel elements, each of "first importance," but he starts with Jesus' death.

Wow! The "first" item of "first importance" is Jesus' death for our sins. If Jesus had not actually died, nothing else matters. Only His death can deal with our sins; His is the one blood sacrifice that works.*

- If Jesus did not die, there's no forgiveness.
- If Jesus did not die, there's was no resurrection.
- If Jesus did not die, there's no need for witnesses of his resurrection.

But Jesus did die, and there were witnesses† of this fact including the apostle John and Jesus' mother.‡

If you leave out Jesus's death then there is no good news.

What is the Sword of the Spirit saying to we who have ears?

---

* Luke 22:20 (NASB) And in the same way He took the cup after they had eaten, saying, "This cup which is poured out for you is the new covenant in My blood.
† The Centurion who made sure Jesus was dead provided witnesses proof of Jesus' death by piercing his side (John 19:32-37). Joseph of Arimathea, member of the Sanhedrin, was a key witness confirming Jesus' death; with the help of Nicodemus (John 19:39), he prepared Jesus' body and buried it in a new tomb (Luke 23:50-53).
‡ Witnesses of Jesus' death mentioned in John 19:25-27 include the apostle John (as the disciple whom Jesus loved), Jesus' mother, Mary the wife of Clopas, and Mary Magdalene.

133
How Much Gospel Is Enough?

Mark 13:9–13 (ESV)

> [9]"But be on your guard. For they will deliver you over to councils, and you will be beaten in synagogues, and you will stand before governors and kings for my sake, to bear witness before them. [10]And the gospel must first be proclaimed to all nations. [11]And when they bring you to trial and deliver you over, do not be anxious beforehand what you are to say, but say whatever is given you in that hour, for it is not you who speak, but the Holy Spirit. [12]And brother will deliver brother over to death, and the father his child, and children will rise against parents and have them put to death. [13]And you will be hated by all for my name's sake. But the one who endures to the end will be saved.

The gospel must be preached. It is the good news about Jesus, but many don't want to hear. The disciples would be beaten, hated, and put to death for preaching it. Some have suggested that they should adjust their message a little bit in order to get "better" results. That's not Jesus' plan.

Jesus knew, long before he lived on earth, how the gospel would be both hated and loved. Jesus' work at the cross — His death burial and resurrection[*] — must be preached, even though some can't even stand His name.

---

[*] The central elements of the gospel message are plainly laid out in 1 Corinthians 15:1-8. They include Jesus' death for the sins of mankind (according to the scriptures), His burial and resurrection (according to the scriptures), and the multitude of resurrection witnesses willing to testify to the truth of the gospel – even to death. Throughout the book of Acts we find that the apostles and evangelists include a call to belief, repentance, confession, and baptism.

The one who endures to the end will be saved. This saved one keeps on preaching the gospel, enduring beatings to her last breath. How long will it be preached?

Revelation 14:6 (ESV)

> Then I saw another angel flying directly overhead, with an eternal gospel to proclaim to those who dwell on earth, to every nation and tribe and language and people.

There will never be an end to the preaching of the gospel. When the heavens and earth are destroyed,* gospel preaching will continue for the eternal glory of Jesus.

What is the Sword of the Spirit saying to we who have ears?

---

* Mark 13:31 (ESV) "Heaven and earth will pass away, but my words will not pass away"

134
Reasons for Envy

Mark 15:6–15 (ESV)

⁶Now at the feast he used to release for them one prisoner for whom they asked. ⁷And among the rebels in prison, who had committed murder in the insurrection, there was a man called Barabbas. ⁸And the crowd came up and began to ask Pilate to do as he usually did for them. ⁹And he answered them, saying, "Do you want me to release for you the King of the Jews?" ¹⁰For he perceived that it was out of envy that the chief priests had delivered him up. ¹¹But the chief priests stirred up the crowd to have him release for them Barabbas instead. ¹²And Pilate again said to them, "Then what shall I do with the man you call the King of the Jews?" ¹³And they cried out again, "Crucify him." ¹⁴And Pilate said to them, "Why? What evil has he done?" But they shouted all the more, "Crucify him." ¹⁵So Pilate, wishing to satisfy the crowd, released for them Barabbas, and having scourged Jesus, he delivered him to be crucified.

Why were the chief priests envious?

Clearly, Jesus' growing power was a factor. Jesus had just ridden into town on a King's donkey (Mark 11:1-7ff). The people correctly recognized Jesus' action, predicted in Zechariah 9:9. Therefore they gave him a royal welcome.

Another source of their envy could be his power to heal the lame and the blind, and to raise the dead. A deeper source of envy could be Jesus' compassion for the poor and his personal humility. When one sees another authentically living out compassion and humility, he cannot help but be envious when he lacks it. Seeing the compassionate actions of another triggers introspection, forcing us to admit our own indifference.

But most of all they are envious of a man without sin; a sinlessness which even corrupt Pilate acknowledged. Being without sin identifies Jesus as God,* for only God is without sin. This moral purity further qualifies Jesus to offer himself for humanity as the unblemished lamb of God during this ultimate Passover feast.

Jesus: let us not envy Him; Let us worship Him.

What is the Sword of the Spirit saying to we who have ears?

---

* Isaiah 53 prophesies that Jesus' would come, die sinless ,and rise again. Isaiah 53:9 talks about his innocence. Jesus Christ the righteous makes the perfect advocate, 1 John 2:1, for us sinners with his Father who is too holy to even look upon sin (Habakkuk 1:13).

135
Echoes of Satan's Voice

Mark 15:26–32 (NASB95)

²⁶The inscription of the charge against Him read, "THE KING OF THE JEWS." ²⁷They crucified two robbers with Him, one on His right and one on His left. ²⁸[And the Scripture was fulfilled which says, "And He was numbered with transgressors."] ²⁹Those passing by were hurling abuse at Him, wagging their heads, and saying, "Ha! You who [are going to] destroy the temple and rebuild it in three days, ³⁰save Yourself, and come down from the cross!" ³¹In the same way the chief priests also, along with the scribes, were mocking [Him] among themselves and saying, "He saved others; He cannot save Himself. ³²"Let [this] Christ, the King of Israel, now come down from the cross, so that we may see and believe!" Those who were crucified with Him were also insulting Him.

The priests and scribes mock Jesus by asking for two things.

First, they ask Jesus to prove his royal power by saving himself. From a worldly perspective, that makes sense; a powerful king had better be able to save himself or else his saving power is worthless.

Second, they ask Jesus to come down off the cross. This would constitute a miraculous sign ("so that we may see and believe").

These statements are demonic because they echo Satan's will. In this sense, you could describe these mockers as possessed.

This brings to mind Jesus' forty days of fasting in the wilderness. Satan tempted him to turn stones into bread and save himself (from starvation). Satan also asked him to perform a powerful miracle, to jump off the pinnacle of the temple. That would be impressive if the angels caught him; Many "would believe".

Rather than echo Satan's will, we must affirm Jesus' will. It was His will to go to the cross.*

What is the Sword of the Spirit saying to we who have ears?

---

* Hebrews 12:2 (ESV) looking to Jesus, the founder and perfecter of our faith, who for the joy that was set before him endured the cross, despising the shame, and is seated at the right hand of the throne of God.

136
The Father's Will and Power

John 18:2–3, 9–11 (NIV)

²Now Judas, who betrayed him, knew the place, because Jesus had often met there with his disciples. ³So Judas came to the garden, guiding a detachment of soldiers and some officials from the chief priests and the Pharisees. They were carrying torches, lanterns and weapons. ...

⁹This happened so that the words he had spoken would be fulfilled: "I have not lost one of those you gave me." ¹⁰Then Simon Peter, who had a sword, drew it and struck the high priest's servant, cutting off his right ear. (The servant's name was Malchus.) ¹¹Jesus commanded Peter, "Put your sword away! Shall I not drink the cup the Father has given me?"

Matthew 26:52–54 (NIV)

"Put your sword back in its place," Jesus said to him, "for all who draw the sword will die by the sword. Do you think I cannot call on my Father, and he will at once put at my disposal more than twelve legions of angels? But how then would the Scriptures be fulfilled that say it must happen in this way?"

Jesus is heading to the cross; the soldiers arresting him are helping him to his goal. This goal, this cup, was given him by his Father. It is both the will of the Father and the Son.

This is the plan, and the Father's will and power are accomplishing it. The Father could have provided twelve legions of angels to prevent this crucifixion. But the Father is applying even greater power, saving power, through the cross.

"For the message of the cross is foolishness to those who are perishing, but to us who are being saved it is the power of God," (1 Corinthians 1:18 NIV).

What is the Sword of the Spirit saying to we who have ears?

137
Signs Upon Signs

Mark 16:19-20 (NASB95)

¹⁹So then, when the Lord Jesus had spoken to them, He was received up into heaven and sat down at the right hand of God. ²⁰And they went out and preached everywhere, while the Lord worked with them, and confirmed the word by the signs that followed.

These last couple of verses in Mark contain signs that help us understand who Jesus is.

1. Jesus had just risen from the dead.*

2. Normally, dead men don't speak; Jesus rose to the occasion.

3. Jesus' ascended into heaven.

4. Jesus was given the place of honor at the right hand of God; he shares that spot with no one.

5. His disciples actually obeyed his command to preach the good news everywhere; that's a lot of authority.

6. Even though he's at the right hand of God in heaven, Jesus is working with his disciples on earth; he can be in multiple places at once.

7. From heaven, Jesus provided the disciples miraculous signs to confirm the message.

Man can't do all this. Angels can't do all this. But Jesus is God.

What is the Sword of the Spirit saying to we who have ears?

---

* Upon rising, He spoke to His disciples over a 40 day period prior to his ascension into heaven. See Acts 1:3.

138
Eternal Glory Found

2 Timothy 2:8–10 (NASB95)

⁸Remember Jesus Christ, risen from the dead, descendant of David, according to my gospel, ⁹for which I suffer hardship even to imprisonment as a criminal; but the word of God is not imprisoned. ¹⁰For this reason I endure all things for the sake of those who are chosen, so that they also may obtain the salvation which is in Christ Jesus and with it eternal glory.

Paul calls it "my gospel" because that's what he preaches. Yet, in the same sentence he calls it "God's" ("the word of God is not imprisoned"). That's because Paul received his good news from God, news that sets people free from sin and death.*

It's good news about the salvation which one finds "in Christ Jesus." It's eternally good news.

But, were one to leave Christ Jesus, they would be outside salvation. That is bad news.

Eternal glory may only be found in the eternal Jesus; he's the one.

What is the Sword of the Spirit saying to we who have ears?

---

* Romans 8:2 (NASB95) For the law of the Spirit of life in Christ Jesus has set you free from the law of sin and of death.

139
Salvation Delivery

Titus 2:11–14 (NASB95)

¹¹For the grace of God has appeared, bringing salvation to all men, ¹²instructing us to deny ungodliness and worldly desires and to live sensibly, righteously and godly in the present age, ¹³looking for the blessed hope and the appearing of the glory of our great God and Savior, Christ Jesus, ¹⁴who gave Himself for us to redeem us from every lawless deed, and to purify for Himself a people for His own possession, zealous for good deeds.

Verse 11 says that salvation has been brought to all men. But not all men are saved, most will remain unsaved.

Though Jesus brought down salvation from heaven, people are rejecting him. Some reject Him because they don't want to deny their fleshly desires. Others reject Him because His salvation doesn't match their expectations.

For whatever reason you might be rejecting His gift of salvation, reflect on the status of the giver. Jesus is not a hero-king from your hometown. He's not from some high order of angels. He who gives Himself is "our great God and Savior, Jesus Christ."

Please don't reject God.

What is the Sword of the Spirit saying to we who have ears?

140
Abide in the Safe Teaching

2 John 1:7–9 (ESV)

⁷For many deceivers have gone out into the world, those who do not confess the coming of Jesus Christ in the flesh. Such a one is the deceiver and the antichrist. ⁸Watch yourselves, so that you may not lose what we have worked for, but may win a full reward. ⁹Everyone who goes on ahead and does not abide in the teaching of Christ, does not have God. Whoever abides in the teaching has both the Father and the Son.

How can that be? How can going beyond the teaching of Christ cause one to lose God?

The first reason is Jesus' teaching itself. His teaching is the way into God's family.* No other way leads to God.†

Before covering the second reason, consider what it means to be "in the teaching of Christ". All Christians should be teaching Christ. But to permit additions to Jesus' teaching is to "leave it". By going on ahead you quit following, you quit being a disciple. Jesus' use of the word "abide" indicates "remaining in," "living in," His teaching. On the other side, to leave out unpalatable parts of Jesus' teaching is not even getting into his teaching to begin with.

The second reason going beyond Christ's teaching causes one to lose God is Jesus himself; Jesus is God. Abiding in Jesus is abiding in God. It is within Jesus that you find God and remain in God.‡

What is the Sword of the Spirit saying to we who have ears?

---

*   John 1:12 (ESV) But to all who did receive him, who believed in his name, he gave the right to become children of God,
†   John 14:6 (ESV) Jesus said to him, "I am the way, and the truth, and the life. No one comes to the Father except through me.
‡   John 10:29-31 (ESV) My Father, who has given them to me, is greater than all, and no one is able to snatch them out of the Father's hand. I and the Father are one."

141
Discipleship to the Death

Luke 14:25–33 (RSV)

²⁵Now great multitudes accompanied him; and he turned and said to them, ²⁶"If any one comes to me and does not hate his own father and mother and wife and children and brothers and sisters, yes, and even his own life, he cannot be my disciple. ²⁷Whoever does not bear his own cross and come after me, cannot be my disciple. ²⁸For which of you, desiring to build a tower, does not first sit down and count the cost, whether he has enough to complete it? ²⁹Otherwise, when he has laid a foundation, and is not able to finish, all who see it begin to mock him, ³⁰saying, 'This man began to build, and was not able to finish.' ³¹Or what king, going to encounter another king in war, will not sit down first and take counsel whether he is able with ten thousand to meet him who comes against him with twenty thousand? ³²And if not, while the other is yet a great way off, he sends an embassy and asks terms of peace. ³³So therefore, whoever of you does not renounce all that he has cannot be my disciple.

A disciple is a follower. Some disciples show more devotion to their teacher than others. Jesus is demanding ultimate devotion from his followers.

Did God, who calls himself jealous,* have a problem with Jesus' words? Not at all. Following Jesus is more important than life itself because Jesus is God.

John 10:30, "I and the Father are one."

What is the Sword of the Spirit saying to we who have ears?

---

*   Exodus 20:4 (RSV) ...for I the LORD your God am a jealous God, ...

142
New Covenant Established

Jeremiah 31:31–34 (ESV)

^{31}"Behold, the days are coming, declares the LORD, when I will make a new covenant with the house of Israel and the house of Judah, ^{32}not like the covenant that I made with their fathers on the day when I took them by the hand to bring them out of the land of Egypt, my covenant that they broke, though I was their husband, declares the LORD. ^{33}For this is the covenant that I will make with the house of Israel after those days, declares the LORD: I will put my law within them, and I will write it on their hearts. And I will be their God, and they shall be my people. ^{34}And no longer shall each one teach his neighbor and each his brother, saying, 'Know the LORD,' for they shall all know me, from the least of them to the greatest, declares the LORD. For I will forgive their iniquity, and I will remember their sin no more."

1 Corinthians 11:23–25 (ESV)

^{23}For I received from the Lord what I also delivered to you, that the Lord Jesus on the night when he was betrayed took bread, ^{24}and when he had given thanks, he broke it, and said, "This is my body, which is for you. Do this in remembrance of me." ^{25}In the same way also he took the cup, after supper, saying, "This cup is the new covenant in my blood. Do this, as often as you drink it, in remembrance of me."

The LORD declared to Jeremiah that He'd establish a "new covenant." Only He is in a position to replace His old covenant. The LORD is powerful enough to make it happen, to fulfill His promise.

So, when did the LORD establish it? The LORD Jesus established it with His own blood at the cross. And, it was powerfully confirmed by the resurrection.

What is the Sword of the Spirit saying to we who have ears?

143
God's Interests vs. Man's

Mark 8:31–38 (NASB95)

³¹ And He began to teach them that the Son of Man must suffer many things and be rejected by the elders and the chief priests and the scribes, and be killed, and after three days rise again. ³² And He was stating the matter plainly. And Peter took Him aside and began to rebuke Him. ³³ But turning around and seeing His disciples, He rebuked Peter and *said, "Get behind Me, Satan; for you are not setting your mind on God's interests, but man's."

³⁴ And He summoned the crowd with His disciples, and said to them, "If anyone wishes to come after Me, he must deny himself, and take up his cross and follow Me. ³⁵ "For whoever wishes to save his life will lose it, but whoever loses his life for My sake and the gospel's will save it. ³⁶ "For what does it profit a man to gain the whole world, and forfeit his soul? ³⁷ "For what will a man give in exchange for his soul? ³⁸ "For whoever is ashamed of Me and My words in this adulterous and sinful generation, the Son of Man will also be ashamed of him when He comes in the glory of His Father with the holy angels."

God's Interests
- Jesus reveals his plan, stating it plainly (8:31–32a)
- Jesus makes a way to join Him via the cross (8:34)
- One is saved by losing his life (8:35b)

Man's Interests
- Both Peter and Satan hate Jesus's plan (8:32b–33)
- Saving one's own skin is Satan's way (8:35a)

What is the Sword of the Spirit saying to we who have ears?

❦ 144 ❦
Truly Knowing Truth

1 John 5:20 (ESV)

And we know that the Son of God has come and has given us understanding, so that we may know him who is true; and we are in him who is true, in his Son Jesus Christ. He is the true God and eternal life.

Pilate once asked "What is truth?"* I doubt that he really wanted an answer. Truth Himself had been standing right in front of him when he mouthed the question.

This letter, 1 John, was written by the apostle to Christians. Unlike Pilate, they know the person who is true.

But just how true can Jesus really be? The record of His life, both in heaven and on earth, can overcome the questions of any serious truth seeker.

Jesus overcomes because "He is the true God..."

What is the Sword of the Spirit saying to we who have ears?

---

* During the trial, Pilate asked the question, "What is truth?" (John 18:38). After asking, he left the presence of Jesus to make another attempt at placating the mob calling for Jesus' crucifixion. It is not clear if Pilate expected an answer or if the question was rhetorical.

Addendum

When sharing Jesus, it is critical to make conversations constructive. Keeping the conversation going is key, it's part of building and maintaining a relationship.

Over the course of those 144 days there were three devotionals contributed by my friend Roger Clevenger. Per usual, these were also addressed to R.M. I included one of Roger's among the 144 (see devotional #55, Atonement). The other two are included here.

The Good News Is God's Power

Romans 1:16 (NIV)

For I am not ashamed of the gospel, because it is the power of God that brings salvation to everyone who believes: first to the Jew, then to the Gentile.

1 Corinthians 15:1–4 (NIV)

¹Now, brothers and sisters, I want to remind you of the gospel I preached to you, which you received and on which you have taken your stand. ²By this gospel you are saved, if you hold firmly to the word I preached to you. Otherwise, you have believed in vain.

³For what I received I passed on to you as of first importance: that Christ died for our sins according to the Scriptures, ⁴that he was buried, that he was raised on the third day according to the Scriptures,

Gospel means "Good News". The message of the cross is good news (gospel), not bad news, nor is it foolishness.

—Roger Clevenger

The Hope of Israel

The final main event in physical Israel's history was the first coming of Christ, prophesied many times in the OT, as summed up in God's words to Abraham and also to Jacob, "in you all the families of the earth shall be blessed" (Genesis 12:3; see Genesis 28:14).

The first coming of Jesus was the main event for which Israel was given a special existence in the first place. The promises originally made to the patriarchs were fulfilled in Christ's coming and especially in His resurrection from the dead (Acts 13:30–34). Of all the events and blessings for which the Jews could thank God, the climatic one, the "grand finale," was Christ's first coming (Romans 9:1–5).

Christ is called "the hope of Israel" (Acts 28:20).

—Roger Clevenger

I hope that sharing these messages with R.M. will contribute to his understanding and ultimately play a part in his becoming a Christian. I pray that my life and words will not obscure God's glory for R.M. or for anyone.

—W. Bascom Moore

Index of Verses

Gen 2:7	78	Ps 102:25-27	186
Gen 3:1-13	113	Ps 102:26-27	174
Gen 4:10	184	Ps 103:13	114
Gen 6:5-8	121	Ps 107:28-30	125, 141
Gen 12:3	219	Ps 110:4	57
Gen 20:7	22	Ps 118:22	72
Gen 22:6-8	22	Ps 118:22-23	36
Gen 22:8	197	Ps 118:25-26	191
Gen 28:14	219	Isa 7:14	39
Exod 4:11-12	139	Isa 8:14	72
Exod 13:18	139	Isa 9:6	133
Exod 16:4	139	Isa 28:16	72
Exod 20:4	214	Isa 29:14	70
Exod 22:26-27	114	Isa 40:3	107
Exod 24:8	8	Isa 53	52, 205
Exod 24:12	137	Isa 53:7-8	30
Exod 31:15	109	Isa 53:9	205
Exod 33:18	176	Isa 53:10	197
Exod 33:20	176	Isa 62:1	119
Lev 14:2-32	115	Isa 62:4-5	119
Lev 19:3	109	Jer 31:31-34	58, 215
Lev 24:16	86	Jer 31:33	60
Num 13:8	38	Jer 31:34	60
Num 13:16	38	Ezek 34:15-16	104
Deut 18:15-20	148	Ezek 34:31	104
2 Kings 5:1-14	114	Ezek 37	63
1 Chr 17:11-14	182	Dan 7:13-14	46
Job 1:6-2	113	Dan 12:13	87
Ps 2	20	Hab 1:13	205
Ps 2:1-2	28	Zech 9:9	190, 20
Ps 2:7	20	Matt 1:20-23	38
Ps 23:1-2	104	Matt 4:10	81, 160
Ps 40:6-8	48	Matt 6:24	160
Ps 41:9	43, 92	Matt 11:27	132
Ps 45:6	108	Matt 16:21-27	13
Ps 45:6-7	186	Matt 22:12-13	163

Matt 24:24	64	Mark 9:1	144
Matt 24:30-31	47	Mark 9:4-8	149
Matt 24:35	69	Mark 9:7-10	27
Matt 25:46	169	Mark 9:16-29	150
Matt 26:39	164	Mark 9:30-32	34, 35
Matt 26:52-54	208	Mark 9:42-50	121
Matt 26:53	51	Mark 10:32-34	35
Matt 28:18	65, 66	Mark 11:1-7	204
Matt 28:18-20	19, 66, 179	Mark 11:7-10	190
		Mark 12:1-12	36
Matt 28:19-20	99	Mark 12:22-27	40
Mark 1:1-4	106	Mark 13:9-13	202
Mark 1:4-8	110	Mark 13:31	203
Mark 1:15	136	Mark 14:3-9	194
Mark 1:23-28	112	Mark 14:17-21	42
Mark 1:34	112	Mark 14:22-26	45
Mark 1:40-44	114	Mark 14:61-64	46
Mark 2:1-12	116	Mark 15:2	167
Mark 2:18-20	118	Mark 15:6-15	204
Mark 2:23-28	109	Mark 15:26-32	206
Mark 3:1-6	120	Mark 15:32	33
Mark 3:5	121	Mark 16:19-20	210
Mark 3:13-19	137	Luke 3:23-38	183
Mark 4:1-12	122	Luke 3:31	183
Mark 4:35-41	124	Luke 7:11-17	63
Mark 5:5-20	126	Luke 9:31	153
Mark 5:27-34	128	Luke 14:25-33	214
Mark 5:38-42	130	Luke 16:27-31	41
Mark 6:1-2	132	Luke 18:31-34	6
Mark 6:7-13	136	Luke 21:8	76
Mark 6:34-44	138	Luke 22:20	8, 201
Mark 6:47-52	140	Luke 22:41-42	24
Mark 7:31-37	142	Luke 23:2	33
Mark 8:29-33	27, 32	Luke 23:50-53	201
Mark 8:31-33	7	Luke 24:1-8	9
Mark 8:31-38	216	Luke 24:13-27	10

Luke 24:36-44	12	John 10:30-33	86
Luke 24:45-47	13	John 11:24-27	87
John 1:1	176	John 11:25-26	19
John 1:12	213	John 11:47-53	88
John 1:14	176	John 12:20-26	90
John 1:29	23	John 12:27-33	91
John 2:18-22	52, 83	John 12:28-33	18
John 2:19-21	183	John 12:32-33	77
John 3:5	180	John 13:13	160
John 3:13	53	John 13:17-19	92
John 3:16	54, 172, 183	John 14:6	97, 198, 213
John 3:31	53	John 14:7-10	93
John 3:35	183	John 14:31	192
John 3:35-36	55	John 15:5	56
John 4:24	180	John 16:28-30	94
John 5:17-18	62, 63	John 17:5	25, 177
John 5:21	63	John 17:15-24	98
John 5:24-25	64	John 17:24	99
John 5:27	167	John 17:26	19
John 6:5-6	67	John 18:2-3	208
John 6:8-11	67	John 18:9-11	208
John 8:12	76, 198	John 18:35-37	96
John 8:23	77	John 18:38	217
John 8:28	77	John 19:6-13	100
John 8:44	199	John 19:10-11	134
John 9:1	78	John 19:25-27	201
John 9:5-7	78	John 19:32-37	201
John 9:32-38	80	John 19:39	201
John 10:11	104	John 20:19-23	95
John 10:17	192	John 20:24-29	102
John 10:17-18	51, 82, 8	Acts 1:3	210
John 10:27-30	85	Acts 1:8	144
John 10:29-31	213	Acts 2:1-3	145
John 10:30	19, 81, 83, 214	Acts 2:22-23	14
		Acts 2:28-41	146

Acts 2:29-31	14	1 Cor 1:18	171, 189, 209
Acts 2:36-37	14		
Acts 2:38	13, 15, 152	1 Cor 1:18-25	70
		1 Cor 1:30-31	132
Acts 2:41	15, 145	1 Cor 8:4-6	173
Acts 3:6-7	16	1 Cor 10:4	67
Acts 3:11-20	16	1 Cor 11:23-25	215
Acts 3:17-18	147	1 Cor 15:1-4	218
Acts 3:17-26	149	1 Cor 15:1-5	74
Acts 3:19	17	1 Cor 15:1-8	202
Acts 3:23	149	1 Cor 15:1-9	200
Acts 4:23-31	28	1 Cor 15:23-25	180
Acts 7:59	151	1 Cor 15:24	179
Acts 8:12	146	1 Cor 15:50	180
Acts 8:26-38	30	2 Cor 3:14	162
Acts 10:26	81	2 Cor 4:1-6	198
Acts 13:26-35	20	2 Cor 5:10	167
Acts 13:27-28	26, 29	2 Cor 11:2-4	135
Acts 13:30-34	219	Gal 3:25-27	152
Acts 13:33	21	Gal 3:26-27	69, 197
Acts 14:13-18	81	Gal 5:17	164
Acts 17:6	165	Eph 1:22-23	183
Acts 20:28	152, 158, 163	Eph 2:8-9	172
		Eph 3:9-11	75
Acts 26:13	199	Phil 2:5-7	176
Acts 26:15	199	Phil 2:5-8	164, 192
Acts 26:15-18	66, 178	Phil 2:9-11	19
Acts 26:18	66	Phil 3:13-14	168
Acts 28:20	219	Phil 3:18-21	170
Rom 1:15-18	188	Phil 3:20	168
Rom 1:16	218	Phil 4:19	169
Rom 8:2	211	Col 1:13-17	143
Rom 9:1-5	219	Col 1:15	93
Rom 9:4-5	174	Col 1:15-17	174
Rom 14:8-9	49	Col 2:8-12	161
Rom 16:25-27	196	1 Thess 4:13-16	130

1 Thess 4:17	168	1 Pet 2:4-10	72
1 Tim 1:17	93	2 Pet 1:11	181, 183
1 Tim 2:5	64, 156	2 Pet 2:1	158
1 Tim 6:13-16	166, 176	1 John 1:7	169
2 Tim 2:8-10	211	1 John 2:1	205
Titus 2:11-14	212	1 John 2:15	61
Titus 3:5	152	1 John 2:22-23	156
Heb 1:1-2	193	1 John 4:7-10	79
Heb 1:1-3	108	1 John 4:9	193
Heb 1:8	108	1 John 5:20	217
Heb 1:8-12	186	2 John 1:7-9	213
Heb 4:15	183	Jude 1:4	64
Heb 5:7	24	Jude 1:4-5	153
Heb 7:20-24	57	Rev 1:4-6	185
Heb 7:21	57	Rev 1:6	183
Heb 7:25-28	50	Rev 14:6	203
Heb 8:8-13	58	Rev 19:7-9	59
Heb 9:15-28	45	Rev 19:9-10	81
Heb 10:5-10	48		
Heb 10:8-10	84		
Heb 10:11-18	60		
Heb 10:14	61		
Heb 11:8	154		
Heb 11:12-16	154, 157		
Heb 11:17-19	22		
Heb 12:2	207		
Heb 12:22-24	184		
Heb 12:28	167		
Heb 13:8	25, 174		
Heb 13:20-21	8		
Jas 4:4	170		
1 Pet 1:1-2	152		
1 Pet 1:3-9	68		
1 Pet 1:10-12	44		
1 Pet 1:11	44		
1 Pet 1:24-25	164		

The Outline of Topics

followed by

The Index of Topics

1. Jesus's Divinity
    - a. Exists before creation
    - b. Jesus the Creator of all
    - c. Jesus came into the world
    - d. Jesus declared to be God
    - e. Jesus claims divine power
    - f. Jesus demonstrates divine power

2. Purpose of Cross
    - a. Fulfill Scripture
    - b. For humanity
    - c. The way into Christ
    - d. Jesus's glory
    - e. Father's glory

3. Cross Plan
    - a. Fulfilled by God
    - b. Accomplished through sinners
    - c. Christ's commission to the church

4. Death, Burial, & Resurrection Predicted
    - a. in O.T. Scripture
    - b. by Abraham
    - c. by John the Baptist
    - d. by Jesus
    - e. by Caiaphas
    - f. by God

5. Premeditated Crucifixion
    - a. Father's decision
    - b. Jesus's decision

6. Essential Cross
    - a. per O.T. Scripture
    - b. per N.T. Scripture
    - c. per Jesus
    - d. Jesus's will
    - e. Father's will

7. New Covenant
    - a. Blood Covenant, Mosaic
    - b. Blood Covenant, Jesus
    - c. Entry into God's Family
    - d. Betrothed to Christ
    - e. Everlasting

8. Kingdom of Heaven
    - a. Predicted
    - b. Jesus is King
    - c. Only one Christ (King)
    - d. No earthly kingdom
    - e. Has arrived
    - f. Eternal

1. Jesus's divinity
a. Exists before creation

John 1:1	176	Col 1:15-17	174
John 17:5	25, 177	Heb 1:8-12	186
John 17:24	99	Heb 13:8	25, 174

1. Jesus's divinity
b. Jesus the Creator of all

1 Cor 8:4-6	173	Heb 1:1-3	108
Col 1:13-17	143	Heb 1:1-2	193
Col 1:15-17	174	Heb 1:8-12	186

1. Jesus's divinity
c. Jesus came into the world

Ps 40:6-8	48	John 8:23	77
John 1:14	176	John 16:28-30	94
John 3:13	53	John 17:15-24	98
John 3:31	53	Heb 10:5-10	48

1. Jesus's divinity
d. Jesus declared to be God

Ps 45:6	108	John 20:24-29	102
Ps 45:6-7	186	Acts 7:59	151
Isa 7:14	39	Rom 9:4-5	174
Mark 1:1-4	106	Phil 2:9-11	19
Mark 1:4-8	110	Col 2:8-12	161
John 1:1	176	1 Tim 6:13-16	176
John 5:17-18	62, 63	Titus 2:11-14	212
John 10:11	104	Heb 1:8	108
John 10:27-30	85	1 John 5:20	217
John 10:30	81	2 John 1:7-9	213
John 10:30-33	86		

1. Jesus's divinity
e. Jesus claims divine power

Lev 19:3	109	Matt 11:27	132

1. Jesus's divinity
e. Jesus claims divine power *(cont.)*

Matt 24:30-31	47	John 5:21	63
Matt 24:35	69	John 5:24-25	64
Matt 26:53	51	John 8:12	76, 198
Matt 28:18	65	John 9:32-38	80
Matt 28:18-20	19, 179	John 10:17-18	82
Matt 28:19-20	99	John 10:27-30	85
Mark 2:1-12	116	John 10:29-31	213
Mark 2:18-20	118	John 10:30	19, 83, 214
Mark 2:23-28	109		
Mark 4:1-12	122	John 11:25-26	19
Mark 6:7-13	136	John 13:13	160
Mark 9:16-29	150	John 14:6	97, 198, 213
Mark 13:9-13	202		
Mark 13:31	203	John 14:7-10	93
Mark 14:61-64	46	John 15:5	56
Luke 14:25-33	214	John 17:5	177
John 1:12	213	John 17:26	19
John 3:13	53	John 18:35-37	96
John 3:31	53	1 Cor 15:23-25	180

1. Jesus's divinity
f. Jesus demonstrates divine power

Matt 25:46	169	Mark 6:34-44	138
Mark 1:23-28	112	Mark 6:47-52	140
Mark 1:34	112	Mark 7:31-37	142
Mark 1:40-44	114	Mark 9:16-29	150
Mark 2:1-12	116	Luke 7:11-17	63
Mark 3:1-6	120	John 1:12	213
Mark 4:35-41	124	John 6:5-6	67
Mark 5:5-20	126	John 6:8-11	67
Mark 5:27-34	128	John 9:5-7	78
Mark 5:38-42	130	John 9:32-38	80
Mark 6:1-2	132	Acts 3:6-7	16
Mark 6:7-13	136	1 Cor 1:18-25	70

1. Jesus's divinity
f. Jesus demonstrates divine power *(cont.)*

1 Cor 10:4	67	2 Cor 4:1-6	198
1 Cor 11:23-25	215	Phil 4:19	169
1 Cor 15:1-5	74	Jude 1:4-5	153

2. Purpose of Cross
a. Fulfill Scripture

Matt 26:52-54	208	John 13:17-19	92
Mark 14:17-21	42		

2. Purpose of Cross
b. For Humanity

Gen 12:3	219	Rom 8:2	211
Gen 28:14	219	1 Cor 1:18-25	70
Isa 53	52	1 Cor 1:18	171, 189, 209
Matt 1:20-23	38		
Matt 16:21-27	13	1 Cor 11:23-25	215
Matt 28:18-20	19, 179	1 Cor 15:1-5	74
Mark 14:22-26	45	1 Cor 15:1-4	218
Luke 9:31	153	1 Cor 15:1-9	200
Luke 22:20	8, 201	Gal 3:26-27	197
Luke 24:45-47	13	1 Thess 4:13-1	130
John 3:16	54	2 Tim 2:8-10	211
John 10:11	104	Titus 2:11-14	212
John 10:27-30	85	Titus 3:5	152
John 11:24-27	87	Heb 7:20-24	57
John 11:47-53	88	Heb 7:21	57
John 12:20-26	90	Heb 10:14	61
John 12:27-33	91	1 Pet 1:3-9	68
John 12:32-33	77	2 Pet 2:1	158
Acts 28:20	219	1 John 2:1	205
Rom 1:15-18	188	1 John 4:7-10	79
Rom 1:16	218	1 John 4:9	193

2. Purpose of Cross
c. The Way into Christ

Matt 22:12-13	163	Acts 20:28	152, 158
Matt 28:18-20	66		163
Mark 8:31-38	216	Acts 26:18	66
Luke 14:25-33	214	1 Cor 1:30-31	132
Acts 2:28-41	146	Gal 3:25-27	152
Acts 2:38	13, 15, 152	Col 2:8-12	161
		1 Thess 4:13-1	130
Acts 8:26-38	30	2 Tim 2:8-10	211
		1 John 1:7	169

2. Purpose of Cross
d. Jesus's glory

John 1:14	176	John 17:24	99
John 2:18-22	52	Rom 14:8-9	49
John 10:17-18	82	1 Cor 1:30-31	132
John 12:20-26	90	2 Tim 2:8-10	211
John 17:15-24	98		

2. Purpose of Cross
e. Father's glory

John 17:15-24	98

3. Cross Plan
a. Fulfilled by God

Matt 1:20-23	38	Acts 13:33	21
John 10:17-18	82	1 Cor 1:18-25	70
Acts 3:11-20	16	Eph 3:9-11	75
Acts 3:17-18	147	1 John 4:7-10	79
Acts 13:26-35	20		

3. Cross Plan
b. Accomplished Through Sinners

Matt 16:21-27	13	Mark 8:31-38	216
Mark 8:29-33	27, 32	Mark 8:31-33	7

3. Cross Plan
b. Accomplished Through Sinners *(cont.)*

Mark 9:30-32	34, 35	John 19:10-11	134
Mark 10:32-34	35	Acts 2:22-23	14
Mark 12:1-12	36	Acts 2:36-37	14
Luke 24:1-8	9	Acts 3:11-20	16
John 8:28	77	Acts 3:17-18	147
John 11:47-53	88	Acts 4:23-31	28
John 13:17-19	92	Acts 13:26-35	20
John 18:2-3	208	Acts 13:27-28	26
John 18:9-11	208	1 Pet 2:4-10	72
John 19:6-13	100		

3. Cross Plan
c. Christ's commission to the church

Matt 28:18-20	19, 66, 179	Acts 1:8	144
		Acts 26:15-18	66, 178
Matt 28:19-20	99	1 Cor 1:18	209
John 17:15-24	98	1 Cor 15:1-9	200
John 20:19-23	95	Rev 14:6	203

4. Death, Burial, & Resurrection Predicted
a. in O.T. Scripture

Ps 2:7	20	Luke 24:36-44	12
Ps 41:9	43	Luke 24:45-47	13
Ps 110:4	57	John 2:18-22	52
Ps 118:22	72	John 13:17-19	92
Ps 118:22-23	36	Acts 2:29-31	14
Isa 53	52	Acts 3:11-20	16
Isa 53:7-8	30	Acts 8:26-38	30
Isa 53:9	205	Acts 13:26-35	20
Isa 53:10	197	Acts 13:27-28	26
Ezek 37	63	Acts 13:33	21
Mark 12:22-27	40	2 Cor 3:14	162
Luke 16:27-31	41	1 Pet 1:10-12	44
Luke 24:13-27	10	1 Pet 1:11	44

4. Death, Burial, & Resurrection Predicted
b. by Abraham

Gen 22:6-8	22	Heb 11:17-19	22
Luke 16:27-31	41		

4. Death, Burial, & Resurrection Predicted
c. by John the Baptist

John 1:29	23	John 3:35-36	55

4. Death, Burial, & Resurrection Predicted
d. by Jesus

Matt 16:21-27	13	Luke 24:1-8	9
Mark 2:18-20	118	John 2:18-22	52, 83
Mark 8:29-33	27, 32	John 2:19-21	183
Mark 8:31-33	7	John 8:28	77
Mark 8:31-38	216	John 10:11	104
Mark 9:7-10	27	John 10:17-18	83
Mark 9:30-32	34, 35	John 11:24-27	87
Mark 10:32-34	35	John 12:20-26	90
Mark 12:1-12	36	John 12:27-33	91
Mark 14:3-9	194	John 12:28-33	18
Mark 14:22-26	45	John 12:32-33	77
Luke 9:31	153	John 13:17-19	92
Luke 18:31-34	6		

4. Death, Burial, & Resurrection Predicted
e. by Caiaphas

John 11:47-53	88		

4. Death, Burial, & Resurrection Predicted
f. by God

Acts 3:11-20	16		

5. Premeditated Crucifixion
a. Father's decision

Matt 26:39	164	Mark 8:31-38	216

5. Premeditated Crucifixion
a. Father's decision (cont.)

Luke 22:41-42	24	Acts 13:27-28	29
John 3:16	54, 172, 183	Acts 20:28	152, 158, 163
John 10:17	192	Rom 16:25-27	196
John 10:17-18	51, 82	1 Cor 1:18-25	70
John 12:27-33	91	Eph 2:8-9	172
John 14:31	192	Eph 3:9-11	75
John 18:2-3	208	Heb 10:8-10	84
John 18:9-11	208	1 Pet 1:1-2	152
John 19:6-13	100	1 Pet 2:4-10	72
John 19:10-11	134	1 John 4:7-10	79
Acts 2:22-23	14	1 John 4:9	193

5. Premeditated Crucifixion
b. Jesus's decision

Matt 26:39	164	Acts 20:28	152, 158, 163
Matt 26:52-54	208		
John 10:11	104	Phil 2:5-7	176
John 10:17-18	51, 82, 8	Heb 5:7	24
John 12:27-33	91	Heb 7:25-28	50
John 14:31	192	Heb 10:8-10	84
		Heb 12:2	207

6. Essential Cross
a. per O.T. Scripture

Deut 18:15-20	148	Luke 24:45-47	13
Isa 53	205	Acts 3:17-26	149
Mark 9:4-8	149	Acts 3:23	149
Luke 24:13-27	10	1 Cor 15:1-9	200
Luke 24:36-44	12	1 Cor 15:1-5	74

6. Essential Cross
b. per N.T. Scripture

Acts 3:17-26	149	Acts 3:23	149

6. Essential Cross
b. per N.T. Scripture *(cont.)*

Rom 1:15-18	188	Phil 3:18-21	170
1 Cor 1:18	171	1 Tim 2:5	64
1 Cor 15:1-8	202	Heb 9:15-28	45
1 Cor 15:1-9	200	Rev 1:4-6	185

6. Essential Cross
c. per Jesus

Matt 16:21-27	13	Luke 24:1-8	9
Matt 26:52-54	208	John 15:5	56
Mark 8:29-33	27, 32	John 20:19-23	95
Mark 8:31-38	216		

6. Essential Cross
d. Jesus's will

Mark 15:26-32	206	2 Pet 2:1	158
Phil 2:5-8	192		

6. Essential Cross
e. Father's will

Ps 118:22-23	36	Mark 12:1-12	36
Ps 118:22	72	Phil 2:5-8	192

7. New Covenant
a. Blood Covenant, Mosaic

Exod 24:8	8	2 Cor 3:14	162
Jer 31:31-34	58, 215	Heb 8:8-13	58

7. New Covenant
b. Blood Covenant, Jesus

Jer 31:33	60	Heb 10:11-18	60
Jer 31:34	60	Heb 12:22-24	184
Luke 22:20	8, 201	1 John 1:7	169
1 Cor 11:23-25	215	Rev 1:4-6	185
Heb 10:8-10	84		

7. New Covenant
c. Entry Into God's Family

Gal 3:26-27	69	1 John 1:7	169

7. New Covenant
d. Betrothed to Christ

Isa 62:1	119	2 Cor 11:2-4	135
Isa 62:4-5	119	Eph 1:22-23	183
Matt 28:18-20	66	Rev 19:7-9	59
Mark 2:18-20	118		

7. New Covenant
e. Everlasting

Acts 13:30-34	219	Heb 10:14	61
Heb 7:21	57	Heb 13:20-21	8
Heb 10:11-18	60	Rev 14:6	203

8. Kingdom of Heaven
a. Predicted

1 Chr 17:11-14	182	Zech 9:9	204
Isa 28:16	72	Mark 9:1	144
Dan 7:13-14	46		

8. Kingdom of Heaven
b. Jesus is King

Ps 45:6	108	Mark 15:32	33
Ps 45:6-7	186	Luke 14:25-33	214
Ps 118:25-26	191	Luke 23:2	33
Isa 9:6	133	John 5:27	167
Zech 9:9	190	John 18:35-37	96
Mark 11:1-7	204	Acts 8:12	146
Mark 11:7-10	190	Eph 1:22-23	183
Mark 15:2	167	Phil 3:18-21	170
Mark 15:6-15	204	Phil 3:20	168
Mark 15:26-32	206	Rev 1:6	183

8. Kingdom of Heaven
c. Only One Christ (King)

1 Chr 17:11-14	182	1 Tim 6:13-16	166
Matt 24:24	64	Heb 1:1-2	193
Luke 21:8	76	2 Pet 1:11	181
John 3:5	180	2 Pet 2:1	158
1 Cor 15:23-25	180	1 John 2:22-23	156
1 Cor 15:24	179	Jude 1:4	64
2 Cor 11:2-4	135	Jude 1:4-5	153
1 Tim 2:5	156	Rev 1:4-6	185

8. Kingdom of Heaven
d. No earthly kingdom

Matt 16:21-27	13	Phil 3:18-21	170
Luke 14:25-33	214	Phil 3:20	168
John 18:35-37	96	1 Thess 4:17	168
Acts 17:6	165	Heb 11:8	154
1 Cor 15:50	180	Heb 11:12-16	154, 157
Gal 5:17	164	Heb 12:28	167
Phil 2:5-8	164	1 John 2:15	61
Phil 3:13-14	168		

8. Kingdom of Heaven
e. Has arrived

Mark 16:19-20	210	Acts 2:28-41	146
Acts 2:1-3	145	Acts 8:12	146

8. Kingdom of Heaven
f. Eternal

Ps 45:6	108	2 Pet 1:11	181, 183
Ps 45:6-7	186	Rev 1:4-6	185
Dan 7:13-14	46	Rev 1:6	183
Mark 16:19-20	210		

www.ingramcontent.com/pod-product-compliance
Lightning Source LLC
Chambersburg PA
CBHW040303170426
43194CB00021B/2871